CW01467879

The Little English Boy

By

Hans Potter
&
Liam McCann

About the authors

Hans James Potter was born in 1933 in Capel, England, descending from a Danish / English background. Growing up he had a passion for literature and photography, and he served in the RAF in Germany during the 1950s as an official photographer. He then spent nearly two decades in Sweden working as the Scandinavian sales. He also taught at language schools using innovative techniques before opening a school in Spain. He studied engineering and, later in life, took business courses at Warwick University before venturing a Swedish housing company in the UK. As he approached retirement, he focused on translating literature as well as collecting books and stamps. He was an amazing raconteur who liked to share his knowledge and experiences. When Hans passed away in November 2011, part of his enormous book collection was donated to Westonbirt School in Gloucestershire (attended by his granddaughter).

Liam McCann was born in Guildford, England, in 1973. He attended Hurstpierpoint College and Staffordshire University, gaining a Bachelor of Arts degree in Sports Physiology and Psychology. He excelled on the sports field, becoming county champion in three field events and swimming to a national standard. Liam then formed a rock band that toured Europe, the group's highlight coming in 2001 when they played to five thousand people. In 2003 he turned his hand to writing non-fiction sports and reference books. He has since had 14 published and is now working on completing an action / thriller series featuring hero Ed Sampson.

By Hans Potter and Liam McCann

The Little English Boy

By Liam McCann

When the Messenger meets the King
In the Lap of the Gods
The Devil's Breath
Rolling Thunder
The Battle of Boxhill

Non-fiction

The Olympics Facts, Figures & Fun
Rugby Facts, Figures & Fun
Cricket Facts, Figures & Fun
The Sledger's Handbook
Born to Dribble
The Revised & Expanded Sledger's Handbook
The European Football Championships
UFOs: Fact or Fiction?
Little Book of Survival
Little Book of the Universe
Little Book of Liners
Little Book of HMS Ark Royal
Grand Prix Driver by Driver
British Lions Player by Player
Brazil Player by Player
Snooker Player by Player
TT Rider by Rider
JFK Conspiracies
The Concise History of World War Two

With Sue Todd

Little Book of the Royal Air Force, Red Arrows Edition

With Andrew O'Brien

The World's Greatest Sporting Rivalries

This book is based on a true story and the authors have endeavoured to retain as much historical accuracy as possible. However, some names, characters, places and incidents are either products of the authors' imaginations or are used fictitiously. In these cases, any resemblance to actual events, locales or persons, living or dead, is entirely coincidental.

This edition © Copyright Hans Potter & Liam McCann 2013

The authors assert the moral right to be
identified as the authors of this work.

All rights reserved. No part of this publication may be reproduced, stored in a retrieval system, or transmitted, in any form or by any means, electronic, mechanical, photocopying, recording or otherwise, without the prior permission of the publisher.

This book is sold subject to the condition that it shall not, by any way of trade or otherwise, be lent, re-sold, hired out or otherwise circulated without the publisher's prior consent in any form of binding or cover other than that in which it is published and without a similar condition including this condition being imposed on the subsequent purchaser.
.
Printed in the USA by Createspace. ISBN 978-1479394104
Cover design by Seamus McCann: www.mccannmedia.co.uk

AUTHOR'S NOTE

Hans Gundelach was killed by a lightning strike on the water off Rügen Island in the Baltic Sea during the late summer of 1999. He died doing what he loved more than anything else since he'd retired: teaching young people how to sail.

His story would perhaps not have been written, and would have remained unknown outside his close family, were it not for me, rather fortuitously, being given access to his papers, flight logs and a collection of audiotapes by a member of his family in Copenhagen. Details of his incarceration at a secret location (probably Farm Hall in Godmanchester, Cambridgeshire) and then his time at Camp 020 (Latchmere House) in the UK due to an unlucky misidentification, which may have been triggered by the machinations of the Abwehr (German intelligence service), have only come to light with the release of papers recently declassified by the British government. This theory seems to fit well with his description of the events that unfolded.

Hans, who one could perhaps describe as a polymath with a first class degree in engineering from Copenhagen's Technical University, also studied metallurgy, photographic chemistry, aeronautics, organic and inorganic chemistry, and geology. His many hobbies included genealogy, stamp collecting, book collecting, sailing, boat design, languages and Viking history.

His survival through many adventures during the war was, apart from having a good measure of luck, in many respects because he used his enclyopedic knowledge to fashion solutions to his problems.

In telling his story I have omitted much of his technical note-taking as being outside the remit of a work intended for the general reader. For example, his exhaustively detailed notes on the steps taken to make an abandoned Hawker Hurricane airworthy would only appeal to aeronautic engineers. Apart from his deep well of knowledge, his decisiveness, and his unhesitating determination to prevail, he was spurred on by a hatred of Nazism. This, together with a steely courage, brought him out of many a tight spot.

Although now a distant memory, I remember talking to him in Holstebro, Denmark, before and just after the start of the Second World War. He always had something interesting to say and I recall one conversation in particular when I sounded off about Hitler. He listened for a moment and then said, "Don't forget, there are a lot more good Germans than bad Germans."

Then, surprisingly, I met him later on in the war in the UK. Like most continentals, particularly the Germans, he always referred to the United Kingdom as 'England', and in translating his notes from Danish I have, in the main, followed this convention.

His family said he never spoke of his wartime exploits, confiding only in his wife, Louise, with whom he enjoyed an extremely close and loving relationship. He even kept his involvement in the Wilhelm Mörz affair secret to the end. It was, after all, a private crusade to establish his loyalty to the Secret Intelligence Service operatives who had doubted him for so long, and which, in the end, remained unknown except to a tiny group of people.

Here then is his story, the story of a true Danish patriot.

CHAPTER 1

The Little English Boy

Hans Gundelach always looked forward to his annual holiday in the sleepy but prosperous little town of Holstebro in Jutland, Denmark. He'd first visited his uncle, a cigar manufacturer, as a youth when he was on term break from the Copenhagen Technical University, but for the past five years he'd only managed to stay with him for a week while on late-summer leave from his post as an engineering officer and pilot in the Danish air force.

As he walked his uncle's little terrier into town, he saw the little English boy messing around on a homemade trolley and collecting windfall apples further up the street. There was a large overgrown orchard on an undeveloped part of the main street where one would normally expect shops to be built.

A lady Hans vaguely recognised stopped and smiled. "Lovely apples this year," she said. "Mr Rasmussen and his grandson come down here several times a week, but Rasmussen gives the surplus apples to Sørensen."

"The experimental pig breeder?" Hans said.

"He feeds them the apples as a treat," she replied with a nod.

Hans glanced back at the boy. "It's a shame we can't afford to eat pork every day."

"Well, there is a war on," she said. "And his pigs are for breeding only."

Hans only ever seemed to meet the boy's mother, Rasmussen's oldest daughter, when she came out to call him in for lunch. Aase was a pretty, dark-haired woman who walked with the fluidity and grace of a dancer. Rasmussen himself was a good friend of Hans's uncle and they often swapped freshly churned butter from Rasmussen's bakery for Havana cigars.

When he saw Hans, the English boy stopped messing around on the trolley outside his grandfather's house and ran over. "We can't go home yet because Hitler has messed things up," he blurted. "My mother and brother are stuck too, but I don't mind because the school here is great."

The boy's broad Jutland patois, no doubt picked up from the Rasmussens' laundry woman, amused Hans, particularly as his Home Counties English was impeccable. He suspected that Aase would have liked to get him home but he didn't say so. For his age (he can only have been about seven) the boy was precociously well informed about the current situation in Europe. He even mentioned being surprised to hear English being spoken on the radio in the kitchen when Mr Chamberlain, Prime Minister of England, had declared war on Germany in the autumn.

Hans recalled him mentioning that he'd found his mother and grandmother tearfully hugging one another and it was then that he'd realised the situation was serious. "We were all packed and ready to go," the boy had said, "but not even the aeroplane could take us home."

Hans sympathised with them. He felt a deep loathing for the German High Command. "You'll be back in England soon enough, young man," he said with an easy smile. "Take my word for it."

"I'm quite happy here," the boy replied. "I've even started making pots from the local clay."

Just along the road to the east of Taarnborg there was a small pottery in the leafy suburbs where one could buy various terracotta pieces. Hans had to admit he'd been quite surprised when he'd been told that the little English boy threw well-proportioned pots and that the girls who worked there saw him as something of a mascot, an honorary potter. Some of the boy's efforts had been fired and were displayed on a shelf with a sign saying 'not for sale'.

That evening over dinner, Hans mentioned this to his family. His story met with some amusement as the Gundelachs knew the boy's surname was actually Potter, which seemed rather apt. Their mood became more serious, however, when Hans explained the awful plight of Aase and her children. They were a family trapped by the war.

Hans's aunt nodded slowly, her face set, grim. "The boy's father returned to England a few weeks ago and he's already been conscripted." She sipped from her coffee, something else clearly on her mind. "I'm worried about the local farmers, Hans. They're relying on agricultural labour from Poland to bring in the crops until our harvesting machinery can be modernised, but the Germans won't allow them into the country because they've also got a serious labour shortage."

Hans knew she'd raise the issue sooner or later. "It will have a big influence on our lives," he replied softly. "They're gradually tightening the noose around our necks. I wish we could do something."

"And our trade with Cuba will also be affected by the war," she reminded him. "We need the best Cuban and Sumatran leaf for wrapping our cigars. We have a good stock at the moment but it'll only last for a couple of years."

They had recently invested in a cigarette-making machine that had arrived from Bristol, England, a few days before the war had started, and they were preparing to manufacture cigarettes from Danish-grown tobacco as supplies of Californian leaf were becoming scarce. Hans knew that production trials had produced cigarettes of a breathtaking foulness and his aunt, with her roguish sense of humour, had suggested they package them in a box with a picture of a pharaoh on the front and sell them to the

The Little English Boy

Germans as genuine Egyptian cigarettes!

One brilliant sunny day, as Hans returned from his walk with the family terrier, he found an official government telegram waiting for him on the hall table. He picked it up and scanned the contents, a prickle of anticipation running up his spine. The telegram instructed him to report immediately to Tirstrup Airfield to the east of the town of Randers. Tirstrup was a small grass airstrip used by private members as well as the Danish military.

The telegram came as quite a surprise. Hans had left his uniform back in Copenhagen and was due for demobilisation in a few days' time. Psychologically he had already resigned himself to becoming a civilian and taking up a commercial engineering position. He rang Tirstrup but couldn't get any information about what was going on. Later, the station commander, who apparently knew his father, left a message saying he would send a car to Holstebro to pick him up.

As Randers was some way from Holstebro, he had plenty of time to pack a few belongings, have a shower and shave. He then drove his aunt out to the tiny village of Sir just north of Holstebro. He'd been meaning to run this errand for a while but hadn't yet found the time for it. They stopped on the way at a flower shop and Hans bought a small bunch of dwarf roses.

Before leaving for Copenhagen he felt compelled to visit the grave of his grandmother, Henrietta Ludovika Gundelach. She was buried in the churchyard of the tiny 13th-century Sir church together with her husband, a teacher and former member of the Danish Parliament, Hans Jorgen Hansen-Sir.

As a small boy, Hans had loved visiting his grandfather's workshop – because it smelled of freshly planed wood – to watch him create his little masterpieces in his retirement. He often fashioned wheelbarrows from exotic wood to present to

12

local farmers who had won awards for their produce. From then on, Hansen-Sirs wheelbarrows were much valued but never used, except as an exhibition piece in the home of the winner – a coveted item of furniture.

On arriving at the tiny Sir church, Hans carefully placed the roses just below his grandparents' black granite memorial stone and bowed his head. He and his aunt then popped inside the tiny church.

While his aunt chatted to the elderly church cleaner, Hans sat at a pew at the rear of the church and, head in hands, contemplated his future. There were dark days ahead. Life, he thought, was becoming terribly unpredictable. The threat from Germany hung over his country like a dark pall of smoke. As an individual, he felt pretty helpless. He couldn't help wondering how the Danes would react if the unthinkable happened.

As they left the church, his aunt turned to him. "It looked odd seeing you sitting there. Perhaps you missed your vocation?"

Hans laughed but didn't reply.

His aunt feigned disapproval. "I'd hoped you'd changed."

She knew that he was a stout non-believer and avoided attending church whenever possible. The family looked on his views with forbearance but, like most Danish families, they were a pretty secular lot.

"I've been wanting to come here to thank her for being there when I was young," Hans replied softly. "She was only part of my life for a short time but she obviously made a huge effort on behalf of the family. I often think of things I should have said to her but never had the time."

His aunt gazed into his steely blue eyes and saw a flicker of emotion flash behind them. She ran a hand through his head of wavy hair with motherly concern, then smiled thinly and broke her baffled silence. "You're hard to fathom sometimes, Hans, but I think you mean well." She rested her hand fleetingly on his arm and marvelled at how handsome he was. "I only hope that when you find the love of your life, you can give her a little of the love you felt for your grandmother."

Her gesture brought a lump to his throat. She was not normally so sentimental. "I never seem to meet the right person," he replied.

His aunt winked. "You'll cross paths with her when you least expect it."

When they returned home, Hans found his uncle in the study smoking cigars with Mr Rasmussen over shot glasses of Gammal Dansk bitters. They were deep in conversation. "I'm sorry for interrupting," he said, "but I have orders to leave for the airfield tonight."

His uncle opened his humidor and removed a box of Havana cigars. "Take this as a parting gift."

Hans thanked him and nodded to both men. He'd hardly left the study when the sound of an engine filtering in from outside told him his car had arrived. He kissed his aunt on both cheeks and waved goodbye from the car.

By the time he reached the Tirstrup administration office, night had fallen. His commanding officer was there to meet him but he didn't explain the note until after they'd eaten a hearty dinner at a local restaurant.

The officer eventually slid a folder across the table. "Read the brief please, Hans," he said formally.

Hans opened the file and read the contents. Despite Denmark being neutral, the air force was making various dispositions and the few aircraft available were being dispersed around Copenhagen. Hans's job was to deliver a Dutch-built Fokker to Kastrup aerodrome in the capital. The administration team had completely overlooked the fact that the Fokker was not cleared for night flying, however. All the same, if he took the assignment he would be able to go home because he didn't live far from the airfield in Copenhagen, but the issue with the night flying embargo meant he'd have to stay overnight in military digs in Randers first.

He thought about the assignment for a minute and then nodded curtly. "Okay," he said, the thought of going home strangely reassuring. "I'll do it."

The next morning he found that the Fokker was only borderline serviceable. In fact it was virtually a museum piece and several of the instruments were not working. However, it was deemed safe to pilot at low level in daylight, and the weather forecast was fine and sunny with a gentle following breeze.

"Don't worry," said the officer with a broad grin. "She's airworthy. And it's impossible to get lost in good weather."

Hans wasn't so sure and he couldn't help feeling uneasy, but he needn't have been so apprehensive. By lunchtime he'd landed at Kastrup after an uneventful flight. His civilian clothes and suitcase caused a bit of a stir among the ground crew, but the rigger who signed the aircraft off said he wasn't surprised at his unusual appearance because there was still a bloody war on. It seemed to be the phrase of the moment. Hans was soon in a car on his way home.

His parents lived in a nice house in its own grounds close to the family home of Professor Niels Bohr, the famous physicist, and the Gundelachs occasionally socialised with the Bohrs. Indeed, Fru Bohr was a wonderful hostess, her cooking sublime. Hans remembered meeting Werner Heisenberg, another physicist, while he was visiting Bohr, and he was delighted to be able to practise his German with the scientists.

Hans embraced his parents warmly and unpacked in his room. There was a photo of another of his aunts on the mantelpiece and he instinctively wondered how they were. She had married a German medical equipment manufacturer and

The Little English Boy

Hans had spent many boyhood summers at their home in Aachen, a predominantly catholic German city on the Belgian border. He found it strange how a simple photo could evoke so many memories of his childhood.

During their upbringing, the Gundelach children had been looked after by a succession of English nannies and great efforts had been taken to ensure they grew up in a multi-lingual environment. Hans briefly attended the English School in Copenhagen, and at Christmas and Easter he attended services in a replica English country church that had been built near the Gryphons fountain, the well-known Copenhagen landmark.

Of the two languages, German and English, the latter was always his first choice. Perhaps it was because of his love of the English classics, or perhaps it was due to the not-so-classic literature like the adventures of Bulldog Drummond, and books such as *The Thirty-Nine Steps* and *Treasure Island*. As a special treat, he was occasionally bought a copy of the English *Hotspur*. As much of his engineering coursework was based on German textbooks on the other hand, he regarded German as more of a technical language.

As he finished unpacking he realised that he'd expected Copenhagen to be different, but everything seemed normal except for the lurid headlines in the daily papers. His impression was that most Danes were vehemently anti-Hitler but that they felt no animosity towards the German people. They seemed to have been railroaded into war and now lived politically suppressed lives in an undemocratic country.

His military service behind him, Hans soon settled into a routine and ended up carrying out general design work on lift operating gear. Life, despite the war raging across Europe, returned briefly to normality and the last Danish peacetime Christmas seemed rather special. Unlike many other countries in Europe, Denmark wanted for nothing, except perhaps a little French wine and Cognac. Spring was most welcome when it eventually came because it had been the coldest winter of recent years.

Hans knew his mother was worried about her sister in Aachen. The anti-Semitism had affected the development side of his uncle's medical equipment manufacturing business as most of the senior design staff were Jewish. The lucky ones had gradually left Germany for America or England but that had left him short-staffed. Hans couldn't help wondering how his uncle was going to overcome these problems.

CHAPTER 2

A taste of the Third Reich

One morning, after the welcome comfort of his own bed and a long and refreshing sleep, Hans went down to breakfast.

His mother poured him a steaming cup of coffee. "I'm expecting a telegram any day now," she said quietly, a trace of fear in her voice. "You're bound to be recalled to the air force because of the war."

Hans shrugged his powerful shoulders. He was enjoying being a civilian and was about to take up a design engineering position with a company called A/S Titan on Tagensvej in central Copenhagen, which was within walking distance of the family home. "I haven't given it much thought while I've been busy with my other projects."

Knowing he was between jobs and the call from the air force hadn't yet come, his mother decided to test the water. "Will you travel down to Aachen to help my sister?" she asked tentatively.

Hans knew she'd broach the subject eventually. "Is this about the staff?"

"Your uncle has a partner in his business," she explained. "He's Jewish but he's managed to avoid registration and doesn't have a big 'J' stamped in his passport. He is living under intense pressure, however, because they're bound to find out about his background sooner or later. German society is rife with informers."

"What can I do about it?" Hans asked with a shrug.

"Hear me out," she replied. "The man is a virulent anti-Nazi.

Before 1933 he appeared in print to warn the country about the men who were getting ready to take over. It is, alas, only a question of time before the SD (Sicherheitsdienst – the German security service) catches up with him, and that means a one-way trip to Ravensbruck Concentration Camp. I want you to take him a first-class train ticket from Aachen to Copenhagen. As Denmark is still neutral, we might be able to help him escape."

Hans rubbed his solid chin and exhaled slowly. "What if they don't let me into Germany?"

"They seem to respect our neutrality, Hans," she said. "Cross-border traffic is still allowed."

Hans wasn't sure it would be as straightforward as his mother thought. "I'm having a meal this evening at one of the Tivoli restaurants with a pilot friend, Tommy Sneum. He'll understand the risks so I'd better run it past him."

Later that evening, Hans waited for Tommy to finish his mouthful before raising an eyebrow. "Well, what do you think?"

Tommy held up his hands and shrugged. "If the air force come calling they're going to wonder where you've got to."

Hans had given this some thought. "I could also miss out on the job I'm after."

"Then it's a no-brainer," Tommy said. "You've too much to lose."

Hans exhaled slowly. "But I'd be able to catch up with the rest of my family. God only knows when I'll see them again."

Tommy sipped from his glass and held out his hand. "A trip to Aachen is extremely risky because of the situation in Germany but I wish you a speedy and safe return."

The next morning Hans started out on the first leg of his long train journey from Copenhagen to Aachen via Hamburg. The journey took him via the Great Belt railway ferry and then on down through southern Jutland and over the German border to Hamburg. The Great Belt ferries were large vessels whose restaurants were famous for their excellent cold tables.

As soon as the train had trundled on board and was secured, Hans headed for the restaurant. Crossing the Great Belt only took fifty minutes so it did not pay to be a laggard. He always indulged in a couple of his favourite Danish open sandwiches, washing them down with a few ice-cold shots of Taffel Aalborg Jubileum snaps and a bottle of Green Tuborg Lager (a distinctly Danish treat).

At the German border station all the passengers had to detrain. This was a wartime departure from having passport control and customs formalities in the carriage itself. Hans's worries about entering Germany proved groundless, although there was a large plain-clothed Gestapo and regional police presence along with their so-called 'chain dogs' (the military police). He had not seen their strange uniforms before, except in books, and wondered how the chains had come about.

A burly passport officer with furtive eyes looked him up and down. "What is the purpose of your trip?"

Hans shivered involuntarily. "I'm visiting relatives."

"Do you intend to write home?" the officer asked.

Hans nodded.

"Don't forget that all post leaving Germany is subject to censorship," the officer said firmly.

Hans thanked him for the information and climbed back onto the train. He had a couple of hours' stopover in Hamburg while he waited for the overnight sleeper to Cologne so he used the time to do a little sightseeing. In between the odd bout of window shopping, he explored two lovely churches set back from the cobbled streets. As in Copenhagen, there was hardly any evidence of the war or Nazi oppression except for the occasional boarded-up Jewish-owned store.

Hans was a keen stamp collector and whenever he was abroad he tried to buy a few representative stamps. He always included a duplicate set to send to one of his nephews, who was also an avid collector. He found a post office and selected some stamps, but he instinctively avoided those depicting Adolf Hitler. He bought a couple of envelopes and sent the newly purchased stamps to his nephew as well as to his own home.

When he arrived in Cologne the next morning, Hans was immediately drawn to the imposing cathedral a stone's throw from the main railway station. He had always been interested in ecclesiastical architecture, although he didn't practice any religion. It was easy to imagine how, in former times, the magnificence and intimidating nature of these buildings held the population in thrall.

Having sent a number of postcards with Hindenburg stamps, he returned to the station for the last leg of his journey. The sleeping cars were comfortable and well appointed, and the girl who served morning coffee was very pretty and pleasant, so he arrived in Aachen feeling relaxed and refreshed.

It was lovely seeing all his German friends and the rest of his family again. The Staffordshire bull terrier, Tjuv (Thief), seemed to know when he was coming and jumped up at him as though he'd only been away for a few hours. He handed over the train ticket that he'd bought in Copenhagen, along with a Danish rullepolse for his aunt. This was a standing order with any visitors from Denmark. Rullepolse, which was unavailable in Germany at the time, is rolled and lightly spiced belly of pork pressed into a form and cooked slowly. It is eaten cold – sliced thinly as part of a Danish smorrebrod repast of open sandwiches – mainly on rye bread. Hans knew his aunt was addicted to it.

He learned that Herr Halflinger (his uncle's senior product developer) had been invited round for dinner before he left in a couple of days. Hans was intrigued to meet the man. He was taking a huge risk so he was either brave or foolish, or both.

Hans's aunt spent the rest of the afternoon in the kitchen preparing roast wild boar that had been shot outside the city walls.

"Can I do anything to help?" Hans asked.

"You can pour the drinks," she replied. "Herr Halflinger will be here shortly."

Hans took the tray into the spacious living room and set it on a coffee table. He turned at the sound of someone knocking on the door.

"I'll get it," his uncle said.

He returned a minute later with Halflinger and introduced him to Hans.

Hans could immediately sense the man's fear. His eyes darted round the room as if he expected uniformed German security police to emerge from the kitchen at any moment. He handed Halflinger a glass, the little man gripping it with both hands and trembling slightly. "Please, sit down," Hans said softly to put him at ease.

Halflinger managed a half-smile but he was clearly unnerved about meeting someone new. "Thank you for bringing me the ticket, Hans," he said eventually.

Hans nodded politely. "Anything to help someone with a grudge against the Nazis."

"If they knew who I was they certainly wouldn't have let me work for the Kriegsmarine," Halflinger said.

Hans raised an eyebrow. "What were you doing for them?"

Halflinger looked around the room again as if needing reassurance that they were safe. "We're developing a new rapid-clearing gun sight for the U-boat fleet."

Hans felt a chill run up his back. "The Atlantic convoys are already taking a battering. If the U-boats are equipped with this technology they'll sink even more Allied shipping. With the US staying out of the war and France falling, only the British will be left."

Hans's uncle sipped from his drink and placed his glass on a coaster. "I've been hearing rumours that the British are only a few weeks from running out of food. If they can't replenish their supplies via those convoys they'll be forced to surrender."

"And that'll be the end of the war," Halflinger said solemnly. "There's no way Danish or any other forces could stop the German advance."

"So that gun sight is critically important to the war effort," Hans said. "How does it work?"

Halflinger wiped a bead of perspiration from his brow and took a deep breath. "The sights they're using at the moment take too long to drain after the submarines have surfaced. If their torpedoes don't sink the ship, they must surface to finish it with the deck gun, but all the time they're on the surface they're vulnerable to attack from the sea or air. There's a rumour circulating that the British have developed a radar system that can detect something as small as a periscope so the U-boats' survival depends on cutting the time they must spend on the surface. We've been commissioned to build a self-draining sight manufactured from phosphor bronze with optics made from special water-repellent glass. It should halve the time the U-boat crews need to load and fire the gun."

"How many people know about the new sights?" Hans asked. "And have you built a working prototype?"

"I have at least a dozen people in my workshop," Halflinger replied, "but I'm the only one who knows the formula for the glass coating. They're testing last year's design in the Baltic at the moment but I've made a number of improvements for the latest incarnation."

"The Allies can't allow German submarines to be fitted with the new sight," Hans said. "You must take the engineering drawings with you when you make your escape."

Halflinger shook his head. "If I'm caught I'll be executed on the spot. I won't take that risk."

Hans fixed him with a steady stare. "Millions of lives could depend on your decision."

"I'm sorry," Halflinger whimpered. "I'll destroy my notes but that's the best I can do."

"Someone on your staff will only continue your research," Hans said. "You must take responsibility and hand the drawings over to the Allies. If they know what they're up against, they'll formulate a response to it."

"Like what?" Halflinger said. "You can't just build something to detect surfacing U-boats more quickly."

Hans shrugged. "I'm not an expert in naval warfare but if the U-boats are only going to be on the surface for half as long, then the allies will need to find them sooner. If, as you suggest, that involves a new radar system, then we must encourage that research. Maybe then the allies will provide the convoys with air support as they approach England. The new Short Sunderland could be used as a spotter aircraft." He paused and finished his drink. "The bottom line is that the British need to see the assembly drawings so they can decide what has to be done to counteract the threat."

Halflinger appeared to consider the proposal but he didn't look confident and dinner was a sober affair, the tension between them palpable.

The next morning dawned crisp and cold. Hans loved early April because summer was on the way. He accompanied his cousin, Grethe, to buy cakes for morning coffee. He loved the smells wafting across the street from the German baker, topped by the heady aroma of freshly baked rye bread.

As they left the bakery, Hans told Grethe he wanted to do a bit of window shopping and would meet her later. He'd seen a pair of black fleece-lined gloves that looked warm and cosy. He managed to barter with the shop assistant and bought the gloves for a very reasonable 85 Reichsmarks. They turned out to be even more comfortable than he was expecting.

As Hans left the shop he bumped into Ilse Hoffsas, the daughter of a family friend. She was very attractive, with startling blue eyes and a stunning figure topped by short blonde hair, so it was no surprise that Hans immediately hit it off with her. As they flirted over coffee and cream cakes at a bakery, Hans suddenly realised he might be falling for her.

Later, while he was looking at cameras in a second-hand shop and thinking he'd like to photograph the lovely Ilse, he was shoved in the back and had the breath knocked out of him. He was held roughly against the plate-glass window at the front of the shop by two plain-clothed bullies who pinned his arms by his side.

The taller of the two had very similar gloves to the ones Hans had just bought. "Your papers!" he barked.

Hans could barely move, let alone show them his papers. They marched him off, ignoring his protests, and led him to a nondescript building a few hundred metres away. They threw him into a cold and lifeless room and searched him. They then took him into an office, forced him to sit on a battered old chair and cuffed his wrists behind him.

The taller of the two was obviously a trained interrogator. He sat down behind the heavy desk and examined Hans's passport for what seemed like an eternity. "So, you say you are Danish?" he said eventually.

Hans nodded slowly. "I am."

The interrogator huffed in disbelief. "You are a Jew!" he said accusingly, his eyes fierce, a small bead of moisture forming on his top lip.

"No I'm not," Hans replied with a shake of his head.

The second man cuffed him behind his ears and sent him crashing to the floor. He then pulled Hans upright before knocking him down several more times. Hans was soon nursing a number of bumps and bruises as well as bleeding from his nose.

Hans feigned losing his composure, which wasn't difficult under the circumstances. "I demand to see the Danish consul," he shouted, "to report this outrageous treatment."

He was immediately released from the handcuffs and briefly entertained the notion that his ordeal was over. However, he was frogmarched out of the office, along a corridor and flung into a small windowless cell with a bare bulb providing the only light. The cell was unfurnished except for a chair, an enamel bucket and some damp rags. The door slammed and he was left alone in surprising warmth. Hans used the next hour to clean himself up but the welts on his face were tender and the blood refused to coagulate.

Suddenly the door opened and a voice shouted: "Get undressed."

Hans tried to protest but it was futile, so he undressed and draped his clothes over the chair. Two men in white overalls entered.

One walked round him and eyed him up and down. "Stand to attention and do not move."

The two men then measured Hans's facial features and entered the results on some sort of chart. They seemed to pay an inordinate amount of attention to his private parts but, thankfully, he wasn't molested or hurt. When they finished, they ordered him to get dressed and left. A few minutes later Hans was escorted back to the office.

The same tall officer was sitting behind the desk. He was sifting through the contents of Hans's pockets, which were laid out on a shallow wooden tray. "Sit down," he said firmly.

Hans did as he was told.

"So, you are not a Jew," the tall officer said.

"I've already told you that," Hans replied.

"Why have you come to Aachen?"

Hans took a deep breath. "I'm visiting my family." He then gave the officer his uncle's name and profession.

The officer fixed him with a steely glare. "You do understand why we have to take precautions. There *is* a war on."

Hans thought about making a sarcastic remark but bit his tongue. It was their bloody fault there was a war on.

"Many Jews are not obeying the laws designed to protect them," the officer continued. "So, please explain why you have post office receipts for stamps and letters to Denmark?"

Hans was tempted to say that this abuse by the Gestapo brought disgrace on the German nation, but he held his tongue once more so as not to exacerbate the situation. "I didn't know it was against your ridiculous laws to send a postcard," he muttered.

The officer inhaled sharply but then appeared to relax. "Take him to the waiting room," he said to a second officer.

Hans was taken to a tiny room with copies of *Fölkisher Beobachter*, the National Socialist newspaper, mounted on sticks along one wall. After some time his uncle's secretary arrived to collect him.

Hans eventually managed to convince his uncle that he'd done nothing to provoke the Gestapo, and his uncle was forced to concede that things in Germany were getting much worse. When he went to bed that night, Hans found it difficult to sleep. The experience with the Gestapo had changed his life. He became determined to do something to help combat the evil scourge of Nazism before Hitler's forces overran the entire continent.

His attitude towards Danish Jews was simple: they were Danes first, a sentiment echoed by the majority of his countrymen. There were differences between creeds, but only in the way that Roman Catholics differ from Methodists. The Nazi attitude towards them was abhorrent. Hans decided to get a copy of *Mein Kampf* to see if he could get inside the warped mind of Adolf Hitler. He then mulled over his future but couldn't reach a satisfactory conclusion and he gradually slipped into a fitful and troubled sleep.

He wasn't prepared in the slightest for the news his aunt gave him before breakfast the following morning.

"Brace yourself, Hans," she said, her voice trembling, her face streaked with tears. "The Germans made a lightning strike overnight and caught out the Danish defences. They were weak and unprepared and they've capitulated. Denmark is now occupied territory."

The terrible news shocked Hans to the quick. It was only 1940 and already most of Europe had fallen to Hitler's Blitzkrieg. He and his aunt drank their coffee in stunned silence before Hans eventually stumbled back to his room in something of a daze. He sat on the edge of his bed with his head in his hands. Shock soon turned to rage, but rage quickly gave way to avenging this terrible injustice. And in that moment, he came to a decision about what he would do.

He'd assumed that Denmark would remain neutral in any conflict but the concept of neutrality was something he found difficult to accept, although he realised it was an unavoidable consequence of being a small and relatively powerless country. He decided he would somehow get to England to fight against Nazism and help free his homeland. The more he thought about it, the more the idea appealed to him.

Hans spent the rest of the morning combing the second-hand shops for a jacket and trousers, and a stout pair of Austrian hiking boots. He finished things off with a black beret and a warm woollen scarf. He destroyed all of his personal papers, except for his passport and driving licence. His tweed plus-four suit was, he decided, far too noticeable, so he decided to leave his suitcase with it and a few other items, stripped of any identifying marks, in a left-luggage locker at the station.

He knew he would have to travel light so he bought a rucksack, a Swiss army knife, a small solid fuel camping stove, a mess tin, and a quality compass. At the stationery shop next to the post office he found a large-scale hiking map covering Belgium and northern France. He then popped into a tobacconist and bought an expensive cigar in a screw-top aluminium tube. As he headed back to his uncle's house he only had one thing on his mind: an early-morning visit to Halflinger's workshop.

CHAPTER 3

Leaving the Third Reich

Hans left his relatives' house with a few pangs of regret because he was extremely fond of his German family. When he bid them goodbye, the parting was subdued. Thinking he was heading home, his aunt tearfully begged him to be careful on the train and not to arouse any suspicion. Hans was convinced she'd realised that things had changed for him, but he knew she didn't have any idea about what he was doing. Being careful took on an entirely different perspective thereafter.

The first thing he did was get rid of his unwanted belongings. He dropped the suitcase at the left-luggage department at the main railway station, then tore up his ticket and threw it in the canal. He watched the little pieces drift under the bridge and spread out like a flotilla on the black water. Burning boats and bridges sprang to mind but he knew it had to be done.

He then drifted through the streets until he came to Halflinger's workshop. There were a couple of architecturally interesting buildings nearby and he made a show of photographing them as if he was a tourist. He was actually scouting the area to make sure he wasn't being watched and hadn't been followed. He expected security to be tight around the workshop because of the top-secret nature of Halflinger's project but a thorough search of the area convinced him otherwise. Sensitive installations often stood out when security went overboard so the Germans had wisely played it down to avoid arousing interest.

After another few minutes he approached the front door and knocked.

A short man with closely cropped dark hair and pale skin answered. "Can I help you?"

Hans nodded. "Hans Gundelach. I have an appointment with Herr Halflinger."

"One moment," the man said. He closed the door and disappeared for a good three minutes. He finally reopened the door and gave Hans a thin smile. "He'll see you now."

Hans was shown into a small entrance hall. It was poorly lit and the doors leading off the hall were all shut. Halflinger eventually trotted down a narrow flight of stairs opposite the front door and held out his hand.

"Nice to see you again, Hans," he said, his sweaty palms betraying his nerves. "Do come up to my office." He turned to the man who had answered the door. "Hans is an important client. Please do not disturb us for any reason."

Hans followed Halflinger up two flights of stairs and was shown into a large and well-equipped study. He marvelled at the rows of shelves sagging under a thousand books, cast his eyes over beautiful models of German ships, and smiled when he saw an array of lenses of various sizes.

Halflinger pushed the door closed and slid a bolt across. "Your being here is most irregular," he stammered. "You're jeopardising our safety."

"You know why I'm here," Hans said flatly. "So I won't be long."

"I'm grateful for the train ticket," Halflinger replied. "But I can't take the drawings with me. I'll be sentencing myself to death."

"Things have changed with the German invasion of Denmark," Hans explained. "It'd be too risky for you to escape with the drawings now. You must give them to me."

Halflinger slumped into a large leather chair behind his desk.

"You're mad, Hans. If you're searched on your way home, you'll be shot as a spy."

Hans leaned over the desk, his tone hinting at the urgency of the situation. "I'm not going home."

Halflinger frowned. "Then where will you take them?"

"The less you know, the better," Hans said. "Then you won't have to lie for me if anyone asks you uncomfortable questions."

Halflinger saw the determination in his eyes and correctly guessed that he was motivated by revenge. He must have been devastated by what had happened during the night. He knew the allies needed the isometric drawings for the gun sight, and also knew that Hans was in a better position to deliver them. How he planned to do the impossible was up to him. He eventually nodded and stood, then crossed the room to a large oil painting of Otto von Bismarck.

He slid the painting aside and flicked through a series of numbers on the front of a concealed safe. He then pulled the door open and removed a thick wad of files and drawings. He spread them across the desk before dropping a tiny microfilm on top. "I'll destroy the hard copies, Hans," he said quietly. "So you only need the microfilm. Now, please leave before I change my mind and have you stopped."

Hans carefully slipped the microfilm into his cigar tube, which would have to be inserted in his behind as a charger later. He then gave the cigar to Halflinger and shook his hand. "You've done your people a great service. Someday they will thank you for risking your life."

As Hans left the building, he made sure he wasn't being followed by stopping at the odd shop and checking the streets in both directions. He then headed for the station and took a slow local train to Liège in Belgium. Because Aachen was so close to the Belgian border, customs and security matters were taken care of before getting to the platform. The border personnel were overstretched and Hans had no problem with his Danish passport. The guards had no interest in his rucksack either, which was a relief as Hans's heart was thumping in his chest and there was a slight redness to his cheeks. He managed to get a window seat, but the view was pretty boring and it was impossible to tell where the border crossing was.

When he arrived in Liège, he was surprised by how big the town was. Until he'd begun planning his journey, he had never even heard of it. He was peckish so he found a bakery. The coffee was excellent, the cream torte superb. He asked the waitress, who spoke good German, where he could board a bus to the small market town of Namur.

For some reason, Hans didn't like travelling on buses. This one had old wooden seats and the atmosphere was thick with cigarette smoke and exhaust fumes that mixed with the stale and sweaty smell of the passengers.

When he arrived in Namur, Hans found a cheap hotel for the night. He removed the microfilm from his rucksack and slipped it between the under-sheet and the mattress. He then headed out to find somewhere to eat. He came across a busy but attractive little place and enjoyed a surprisingly good meal of Wienerschnitzel and chips. He had often been told that Belgian chips were the best because they were fried in horse fat. Whether or not this was true, the chips were extremely good.

He noticed a lot of military activity in the small square opposite. The soldiers marching through the town looked so young that they must have been conscripts. They wore ill-fitting uniforms and boots that seemed too big. He tried not to appear too interested in them and finished his meal. Then he sauntered back to the hotel via a café serving coffee and traditional Belgian chocolate.

The next morning, Hans took the usual slatted-seat bus to Florennes, and from there he caught another local bus to Philippeville. The bus to Philippeville was a bit of an ordeal as a largish middle-aged woman got on at the first stop and sat next to him. She was carrying four live hens that were tied up by the legs. Every now and then the birds struggled and filled the air with feathers.

Hans was glad when the journey was over. He couldn't help wondering if those wooden seats gave the Belgians piles. There didn't seem to be any buses from Philippeville so he hiked for what seemed like an eternity to Sautour and then struck out south across the countryside. He planned to hike for a couple of days before slipping into France away from the heavily guarded border crossings. His map showed a lot of forest and open countryside between him and the border.

As he trudged onwards, he couldn't help wondering if he was doing the right thing. Here he was in occupied enemy territory with a top-secret microfilm trying to make it to England. He kept telling himself that he'd make it to the coast and escape on a small fishing boat but every so often, particularly when the going became tough, the doubts would creep in. It only needed someone to challenge him and he'd be discovered. Death was one mistake away. What would his family think of him when they found out?

After several hours he was exhausted. He hadn't yet broken in the new hiking boots and his feet were uncomfortable. He'd also run out of water. Dusk was falling and he hadn't seen a single sign of life for ages. And it had rained the previous night so there was no chance of finding a dry spot in which to curl up.

He was still thinking about what to do when a robust farmer with wispy blonde hair, callused hands and a sun-weathered face appeared from nowhere. Unfortunately, he only spoke French and Flemish but Hans managed to get him to understand that he needed some food and a bed for the night.

"Are you German?" the man asked in Flemish.

Hans shook his head vigorously. "Dansk," he said, repeating it several times. He wasn't sure if the man understood so he showed him his passport as well.

34

This seemed to satisfy him and he led Hans through a copse and across a couple of fields. He lived in a large farmhouse surrounded by outbuildings and an extensive orchard with several beehives. The man beckoned Hans into the cosy kitchen and poured him a mug of strong coffee. He then handed him a plate of spicy pork sausage and coarse brown bread. Hans washed it all down with a strong sweetish brown beer.

The family introduced themselves as Edvard, Agnes and daughter Louise Walraven. Thankfully, Louise spoke excellent English so communicating with them was relatively easy. Hans couldn't help noticing how exhausted they all looked, particularly the two women.

Reaching into his jacket pocket, he produced his Danish passport and some Belgian francs that he'd changed at the bank near the station in Aachen. "How much for the meal and a bed for the night?" he asked. "Just some straw in a barn would be fine."

The family spoke rapidly in French before Louise pushed his outstretched hand away. "We do not want your money. In exchange for a nice bedroom in the main house, will you help us tomorrow? My father is shorthanded on the farm because my brothers have recently been conscripted into the Belgian army."

"I've never worked on a farm before," Hans replied a little sheepishly. He didn't want to stay too long with the family in case the Germans found out what had happened back in Aachen and gave chase.

"If you want a bed for the night, you'll have to learn fast," Edvard said.

Hans had no option but to take up their offer. He would only have suffered needlessly in the cold under the stars if he'd refused. "Then I'm at your service," he said with a polite nod of his head.

"It's easy to understand but quite hard going," Louise explained. "You'll need to unclamp the sugar beet, then trim it

35

and load it onto a cart. The cart is driven a couple of kilometres to the offloading point, where the beet is washed and weighed and eventually loaded onto lorries heading for the sugar processing factory. The factory is running behind this year because the beet should have been delivered at the same time it was harvested."

Hans nodded, taking it all in.

"My dad tried to get both my brothers deferred," she continued, "but he had no luck. I've had to give up college to help."

Hans realised the poor girl was having to do the work of two men. No wonder they all looked exhausted. With the deal struck, he went to bed. He was worn out by all the hiking and the Walravens clearly needed some rest too.

The next morning Hans felt refreshed. After a hearty breakfast, and with the greenery steaming in the warmth of the early morning sun, they all rode in the horse and cart to a nearby field. Hans saw a beet clamp about thirty metres long. It was full of beet that must have been harvested earlier. Hans had to shovel the earth off the clamp to expose the beet underneath. Despite the soil being fairly light, it was backbreaking work because he wasn't used to physical labour.

Agnes and Louise cleaned the soil from the beet and cut off the newly sprouted shoots, which were saved in a large wicker basket for the pigs. Louise kept some of the more lush shoots for the family table. The beet was then thrown onto the cart. It took about an hour to fill the cart and then Edvard drove off. He arrived back after about three quarters of an hour with the muscular carthorse, Klompe, steaming from the effort.

Edvard told Hans that Klompe had originally come from Holland and he was now part of the family. There was no let up in the work. While the cart was away, there was plenty to do to prepare for the next load. It was noon before they stopped for a break but they only had time to eat a little bread and sausage and drink some homemade beer.

Although he was desperate to make a dash for the coast, this was Hans's routine for several days. To begin with the physical work left him with aching muscles – bits of his body he never knew existed made themselves felt – but gradually he got used to the effort. The physical labour was, he realised, toning his body and doing him good. His eagerness to press on was taking a backseat for now. His apathy coincided with a lull in the fighting according to the news on the kitchen radio.

Hans looked forward to relaxing in the warm kitchen after a hard day's graft with a mug of Belgian hot chocolate. When they'd eaten, the family routinely discussed the radio bulletins and the progress of the war, or, rather, its present stagnation. As the days passed, he found himself becoming quite fond of the hard working and loyal Louise.

Although not beautiful in the classical sense, she was slightly above average height and her work-tanned face was bursting with character and had a light dusting of freckles that were brought out by the sun. She had an attractive and lithe figure with ample bosom. When she smiled, tiny crow's feet appeared at the corners of her eyes, which he found quite captivating. She also had a habit of throwing her head back when she laughed, her long brown hair shimmering in the spring sunshine. He loved the way she reasoned, and with her intelligence and ready wit she always had something sensible to say.

Hans, of course, had several girlfriends in Denmark in his air force days, but none of these liaisons had developed into anything deeper, perhaps because life as a pilot had been pretty hectic. During these relaxed evenings in the kitchen, he and Louise chatted about the events that had enveloped them. Her parents understood much of their conversation and were aware of the growing rapport between them. Indeed, they seemed to welcome it.

Hans, meanwhile, was picking up some French, although when they spoke in Flemish it was much easier for him to understand. He realised that Edvard was a quiet and thoughtful man, although he maintained a powerful and rugged physique despite being well over fifty years old.

It took some time before Edvard warmed to his new lodger, partly because of the language problem and partly because he was an insular man with old-fashioned views. The breakthrough in their relationship came when he invited Hans to go out vermin shooting. Rabbits and hares were pests that had to be kept under control, but they were also an important source of food for the family.

Edvard gave Hans a single-barrelled Belgian 12-bore shotgun, which was old but quite serviceable. The family owned a lot of land and always went shooting on Sundays, although occasionally it was called off if the wind direction carried the sound of the gunshots to the nearest village. Because of the influence of the church, it was taboo to hunt on a Sunday or, for that matter, to do any work at all. Most of the time, however, it was possible to hunt over the weekend because the farm was so remote. Hans got the feeling that the family considered religion a nuisance, a point of view with which he was familiar.

Hans always collected the spent cartridges because Edvard recharged them in a workshop in an old bogie-less railway carriage that housed an incredible range of tools. As their shooting evenings became a permanent fixture, Edvard gradually warmed to Hans. He was impressed with the way he handled the guns and was secretly pleased that the Dane had been able to help on the farm for several weeks. A bond of trust had grown between them.

Despite a nagging feeling in the back of his mind that he should be moving on, Hans's feelings for Louise were becoming uppermost in his mind. Initially, he managed to keep his fondness for her hidden because he couldn't see them having a future in a world ravaged by war but while he was helping her over a fence one evening his emotions got the better of him. He took her hands and kissed her gently on her lips. He was delighted when she returned his passionate advance and the kiss lingered until they were both pleasantly breathless.

Neither of them said anything about what had just happened – they were both somewhat surprised – but Hans knew that something indefinable in his life had happened. An incredible elation gripped him and would not subside. His emotions, somewhat predictably, then engaged in a battle of conscience with his sense of duty. The microfilm with the gun sight drawings had to find its way into the hands of the British, but that seemed impossible at the moment.

A few days after that first kiss, Louise slipped into Hans's bedroom in the middle of the night and climbed in beside him. "I've come to tell you I've fallen in love with you," she whispered.

"And I you," he replied softly.

They kissed with exquisite tenderness. This mutual passion was, it seemed, boundless until they eventually drifted off in each other's arms. They woke simultaneously as the grey streaks of dawn dappled the curtains.

Before tiptoeing back to her room in the morning, she whispered in his ear, "Thank you for loving me."

He winked back. "I can't help the way I feel."

When they stopped work at lunchtime, Louise waited for her parents to head back to the house before she sidled over and took Hans's hand. "You've made me so happy," she said tenderly. "But tonight I want you to have me properly."

Hans had not consciously refrained from sex during their first encounter. He had been so overwhelmed with a mixture of love and exhaustion that he'd forgotten about the sexual part of the liaison – something he wouldn't have thought possible – and fallen asleep. He wanted to chastise himself because his selfishness and weakness were allowing him to fall in love. If only he could have stifled his feelings in the early stages of the relationship! In the long term this was bound to cause them heartache. He simply had to move on, but leaving Louise was going to be a terrible wrench for both of them.

Although a little naive about a few of the intimacies of sex, he realised on the second night that Louise was not a virgin. When they were working on their own the following day, he shyly broached the subject.

"I was engaged to the son of a rye farmer from Sautour," she explained. "We planned to marry last summer but fate intervened." She lowered her eyes, her face grim. "He was killed in a tree-felling accident just before the wedding." She paused for a moment before lifting her eyes to meet his. "After the accident I thought my life was over. For months I imagined hearing his motorcycle but he never came. I immersed myself in work but it was only when you arrived that I finally snapped out of the misery."

"Did your parents understand what it was like for you?"

"They supported me as best they could," she replied, "but their sympathy only seemed to make matters worse."

Hans thought that might be why, even when they'd realised that Louise and he were in a relationship, they'd raised no objection. She was an entirely different girl now, with a *joie de vive* and sparkle Hans hadn't noticed when they'd first met.

One night, while they were lying in bed together, Hans decided to tell her what was on his mind. "I'm afraid I'm going to have to leave soon, my love."

"Why can't you stay here?" she gasped.

"If the Germans occupy Belgium and they catch me I'll be shot as a spy," he replied. "It's too dangerous."

Her sobs as she hugged him were heartbreaking.

"Louise," he said, "I give you this promise from the bottom of my heart: if I survive the war, no matter what the future has in store, I will return and spend the rest of my life with you."

Her convulsive sobbing subsided briefly.

"And when I return I want you to be my wife," he added.

"Do you really mean that?" she said, her eyes glinting in the moonlight.

"It is my dearest wish that you shall bear my children," he whispered. As he cradled her in his arms, she eventually stopped crying and drifted off to sleep.

The next morning while they were at breakfast, Edvard stood transfixed by the radio, his big bowl of warm milk untouched. The Germans had amassed troops at the border overnight. It looked as if the invasion had already started.

He'd also realised it was time for Hans to go. He held out his tough farmer's hands. "Thank you for all your help, Hans."

"I'm the one who should be grateful," Hans replied, not forgetting to mention the promise he'd made to Edvard's daughter.

Edvard thanked Hans again and gave him a great bear-hug. "In return for all your help," he said, "I insist on driving you to the French border."

Hans's goodbye embrace with Louise was long and tearful for them both. "Please remember, this is not goodbye," he reminded her. "I'll be back soon."

Agnes was also crying. She gave him a big farewell hug and handed him some food wrapped in a linen cloth. The family did not own a car, but Edvard had an old BMW motorcycle and sidecar combination that was once owned by the police. Using his mechanical engineering skills, Hans had serviced the motorbike the week before.

"We'll ride most of the way through the forest along the firebreaks," Edvard explained. "The BMW twin is relatively quiet but we'll need to keep an eye out for border patrols."

Hans decided to travel lighter than ever, leaving nearly everything with Louise for safekeeping. They left just after breakfast and headed along a metalled road for about ten kilometres before they turned onto the forest track. The ride had been fairly smooth but it became quite bumpy when they got onto a firebreak. Thankfully, the sturdy BMW took everything in its stride.

On a rare stop for a snack, Hans heard a few planes overhead but their engines were muffled by the tree canopy. He guessed the fighters were flying low along the border but knew they'd be incredibly difficult to spot in the trees. The two men finished their snack and climbed aboard the BMW. Further progress was slow because of the unevenness of the terrain but after three or four hours, Edvard suddenly turned ninety degrees and brought the engine down to idle. When they were about fifty metres from the track, he cut the engine and signalled for Hans to be quiet.

They sat in silence with only the tick-tick of the cooling bike engine for company. Hans had not seen anything but he could now hear the pounding of horses' hooves gradually fading into the distance. The men used the brief break to have a final snack and drink.

Edvard grabbed a flagon of homemade beer, half a loaf of bread, some sausages and a few hardboiled eggs from his bag. He wouldn't allow Hans to open Agnes's food pack because he knew he'd need it later. The sight of all the food made Hans realise he was ravenous and they got stuck into their late lunch.

Hans took a final mouthful and washed it down with a swig of beer. "Edvard, I don't know how to thank you," he said.

Edvard gripped him by the shoulder and winked. "Just make sure you come back for my Louise."

Before they started off again, Edvard crept back to the path.

He soon jogged over with four fingers raised to let Hans know the size of the patrol. They then climbed aboard the motorbike and eased it back onto the firebreak. The track eventually levelled out and Edvard accelerated. When the trees thinned, Edvard coasted to a stop and pulled onto the verge.

"This is as far as I dare come, Hans," he whispered. "The French border is about a kilometre ahead."

A stiff Hans clambered out of the sidecar and helped Edvard push the combination around so it faced the way they had come. "I'll keep out of sight in the bushes as I approach the crossing."

Edvard gripped him in another hug and slapped him on the back with fatherly affection. "Bonne chance, mon ami," he said.

Hans, his eyes full of tears, thanked him as best he could.

Edvard started the BMW and slowly drove away. He turned to wave a couple of times and then he was gone.

Hans took a deep breath and set off into the unknown.

CHAPTER 4

France

Hans trudged towards the border along the edge of the path. After a short distance, he noticed a marker post at the side of the track and realised he had entered France. He carried on, alert to any sound or sight of border guards. He was either lucky to avoid them or there were none patrolling the immediate area. The landscape gradually opened out and he found himself crossing fairly flat countryside. He pressed on until darkness fell.

Exhausted, he looked around for somewhere to shelter for the night. After what seemed like ages, he spotted the outline of a straw stack at the edge of a big field. He went round to the rear and burrowed in. The straw was fresh and dry and he soon hollowed out a comfortable bed. He was asleep in no time at all and only woke once when a screech owl startled him. When he realised what it was, he felt strangely reassured and dropped back into a dreamless sleep.

In the morning Hans spent some time carefully picking the straw from his hair and clothes. He didn't want to draw attention by appearing itinerant. With the new dawn came painful pangs of hunger so he breakfasted on the food Louise's mother had given him. Feeling sated he was ready for the new day.

The area where he had spent the night seemed pretty isolated, but after crossing two open fields he came upon a small country road that ran southwest to northeast. After walking for about four hours, he came to a collection of cottages that included a bakery/café.

The tiny establishment was deserted save for a morbidly obese woman who seemed to be in charge. Hans eventually got her to understand that he wanted some coffee and something to eat. She ushered him to a table at the rear, where a scruffy tabby cat joined him. He tickled it under the chin and soon had it purring like a low-flying Messerschmitt.

The woman brought him a pot of black coffee and some sort of plaited cake. He must have looked hungry because she also produced a long pork pie, which he demolished in seconds. As he made a start on the cake, a small boy turned up with a dilapidated wicker basket. The woman filled it with bread and sent him on his way.

The coffee was strong and just to Hans's taste, which was surprising given the paucity of his surroundings. He didn't want to rush as he was appreciating the mid-morning warmth but he eventually asked for the bill by pretending to write on his hand. The woman had no idea what he was doing so Hans removed a 100-franc note and waved it in front of her.

She immediately disappeared into the back gabbling twenty to the dozen before returning with his change. As it added up to nearly a hundred, his meal must have been extremely good value. As he was leaving, the woman gesticulated wildly and muttered something about Le Bosche. Hans beat a hasty retreat, concerned that his lack of French and the news blackout could compromise his security. The microfilm in his rucksack seemed to be getting heavier and heavier.

As he trotted off down the road, he realised he missed the kitchen radio back at the farm, but he tried his best to repress all thoughts of Louise. Leaving her had left an aching void in his heart that threatened to overwhelm him. He vowed to return to her as soon as he'd handed the vital gun sight information to the English.

The road leading out of the village was narrow. He passed the odd horse and cart but guessed that plenty of larger vehicles must have used the road because it was littered with branches from the trees at the roadside. He had to dive into the roadside ditch on several occasions when low-flying aircraft approached. They were nearly all German judging by the sound of their unsynchronised engines. They obviously had control of the skies but he had no idea how far they had advanced. At one point he thought he heard the faint sound of a Merlin engine but he decided it was wishful thinking. He certainly heard the rumble of artillery shells exploding in the distance.

He walked on until well after sundown before looking for somewhere to rest. Sometime after midnight he stumbled into a tiny village cloaked in the inky darkness. He heard sporadic small arms fire in the distance but it was difficult to judge its direction.

The village was suddenly lit up by a green flare. By the ghostly light he noticed that some of the street doors were hanging open. The only explanation was that the village had been evacuated. After tripping over a dead horse, he slipped into one of the larger houses. By the light of a match, he spotted an abandoned meal on the kitchen table. He sniffed the full carafe of red wine and emptied it in a few satisfying gulps. It tasted a little flat but left him feeling light-headed.

He tiptoed up a flight of stairs by the light of a candle he'd found on the kitchen dresser. The beds were made up in each of the bedrooms. A second flight took him up to a huge granary/loft that was filled with assorted junk. He retraced his steps and took the blankets and pillows from one of the rooms and prepared a makeshift bed behind a pile of boxes and old suitcases at the back of the loft. He didn't want to be taken by surprise if the owners returned in the morning and found him downstairs.

Hans soon drifted off to sleep. He dreamed about being involved in a fire-fight, which woke him with a start. The luminous dial on his wristwatch told him it was just after five in the morning. It sounded like there was small arms fighting in the streets below, the noise interspersed with the occasional grenade blast and the deep staccato rumble of a Spandau heavy machinegun.

Suddenly there was a tremendous explosion and rattle of loose detritus from downstairs. This was soon followed by the sound of German voices. Hans inhaled sharply and froze, his ears straining to catch the slightest sound. He didn't know how long he was primed for fight or flight but he eventually became so exhausted that, incredibly, he fell asleep again and only woke a couple of hours later.

The fighting seemed to be a bit further away now. He waited for ten minutes in case there were still Germans in the house, but when he didn't hear any unusual sounds he crept down to the first floor. Glancing into one of the bedrooms, he was shocked to see a German NCO sitting on a chair in front of the open window. He was about to beat a rapid retreat when something odd about the scene struck him. The man was so still he seemed lifeless.

Keeping away from the window, Hans skirted the room and saw why the German was sitting motionless. He was stone dead. A bullet or piece of shrapnel had pierced his skull just below his left eye but there was very little blood. Hans grabbed the chair and pulled it away from the window. The body was still warm. Hans took a Walther P38 pistol from the man's holster in case he was surprised by anyone and then searched the corpse. He found several boxes of pistol ammunition and a couple of full magazines in a leather pouch on the NCO's belt.

Hans also found some banknotes in his wallet, of which he only took the French francs, and a new pair of binoculars on top of a big and surprisingly clumsy green field radio on the floor by his feet. The faint sound of white noise coming through the headphones told him the transceiver was still switched on. He decided to leave the radio alone and get out of the house in case anyone came to find out why the spotter had fallen silent. He was about to leave the room when he noticed another box underneath the spotter's chair. He opened it and found a huge stash of English five pound notes. He knew the Germans were trying to forge them so he took a thick wad and dropped them in his rucksack.

He jogged downstairs and slipped out of the front door into watery sunshine. The deserted street was littered with the debris of war so he decided to head for the countryside. He'd almost cleared the village and was feeling a little more secure when a couple of shots whizzed past his head and had him ducking for cover.

"Hands up!" barked a German paratrooper who appeared at he roadside in his distinctive uniform and helmet.

Hans did as he was told, his heart pounding uncomfortably in his chest.

The paratrooper motioned Hans into a courtyard with a sideways wave of his machine pistol. A British-built Bedford lorry was waiting inside. A group of men were handcuffed together lying in the back of the lorry. Hans glanced around to assess the situation but realised immediately that there was no chance of making a run for it. He'd have to try to bluff his way out of trouble.

"Why is an English soldier wearing civilian clothes?" the paratrooper asked in broken English.

"I am a Danish student," Hans replied in German.

The paratrooper chuckled nastily and heaved him up onto the lorry. Then he handcuffed his wrists to the ankles of the nearest prisoner. He threw a couple of shovels in along with Hans's rucksack, which he seemed to have forgotten to search. The paratrooper climbed into the passenger seat and they were soon bumping along the main road.

Hans glanced at the shovels and shuddered. He might be living his last minutes. He was so angry at how easily he'd been picked up.

After about twenty minutes the vehicle turned off the road onto an exposed heath and pulled up. As soon as they stopped, Hans heard the roar of a high-powered aero engine. He ducked down as the aircraft thundered overhead and strafed the truck with a deadly stream of machinegun fire.

Hans only caught a glimpse of the plane but he immediately identified it as a German BF109. The pilot clearly hadn't bothered to confirm the identity of his target, which was one of the hazards of modern warfare. Within a few seconds the Messerschmitt had disappeared behind a distant ridge. A couple of prisoners at the front of the lorry had been mortally wounded and several others were moaning, but the cab had borne the brunt of the strike and there was no sign of life upfront.

Hans was thankful that the aircraft hadn't been fitted with cannon because their shells were far more destructive than the small-calibre machinegun rounds. Everyone who was alive lay in stunned silence for a few minutes.

Hans motioned to the man he was cuffed to. "We need to get out of the lorry in case he comes back," he said in his limited French.

It was difficult and painful but they had no choice. The steel restraints bit into their flesh but they managed to synchronise their movements and they soon fell to the ground. They then edged towards the passenger door of the cab. Both of their captors appeared to be dead. Hans wrenched open the door and the paratrooper fell out with his Schmeisser machine pistol clutched across his chest. Hans found the key to the cuffs on a chain attached to his belt and quickly freed the survivors.

One of the paratroopers began to moan so Hans reluctantly finished him off with a single shot from the Walther P38. There was no danger of the driver coming round; the top of his head was missing but, rather oddly, his field grey forage cap was untouched. Hans ignored him and checked the vehicle. The cab may have been badly damaged but the truck was drivable.

Hans found a long twig and dipped it into the fuel tank. It was half full and appeared to have survived intact. It took a while to remove all the glass and the driver's remains from the cab. Hans took the wallets from the bodies and shared out the banknotes. He then checked the Schmeisser, set it to single shot and fired it into the air to make sure it was in good working order.

They also took the Mauser rifle from behind the driver's seat but it only had one full magazine. Hans was thankful that he'd paid attention in the Danish air force small-arms familiarisation course because he was now putting that knowledge to good use.

The motley group of survivors, beset with communication problems, eventually reached a consensus that they should use the lorry to get clear of the area. Hans pulled on the driver's jacket and cap and volunteered to drive. The Frenchman to whom he'd been cuffed slipped into the other German's uniform and acted as his co-driver.

He held the Schmiesser machine pistol in the ready position by his side in case he needed it at short notice. They agreed to take the two dead French prisoners but to leave the two Germans. Using the shovels they scraped a shallow depression and quickly concealed the bodies. Hans knew they wouldn't get far on half a tank of petrol but he climbed behind the wheel and started the engine.

He looked over his shoulder into the back and pointed to the sky. "Watch out for enemy aircraft. Shout at the first sign of trouble. It'll give me time to get this thing off the road."

They set off to the southwest and bounced along the narrow road. After about half an hour they found it almost blocked by the wreckage of a German convoy of trucks and horses that had recently been shot up. As they weaved through the carnage, a guard brandishing a rifle appeared and waved them to a stop.

"What are you doing here?" Hans asked brusquely in German to try to bluff his way through.

The soldier puffed his chest out and peered at the truck. "I've

50

been ordered to guard the wreckage until a salvage crew arrives. I'll have to detain your vehicle because the salvagers will need every set of wheels they can get." He cocked his head at the two Frenchmen in the back. "Are these men your prisoners?"

Hans nodded.

The soldier pointed to Hans's weapon. "Shoot them. We need that truck."

Hans had no alternative. He raised the Walther and pointed it at one of his fellow prisoners. The look of abject terror on his face would be an image Hans could bring to mind for the rest of his life. Hans simply winked and then, in a lightning motion, he whirled round and shot the German point blank.

This seemed to cause much consternation amongst the Frenchmen but for Hans it had been unavoidable. He would never shoot an unarmed prisoner, especially an ally, but an occupying German soldier was a different matter. He repeated over and over in his mind that these people were the enemy. They were threatening his way of life and the lives of his friends and family and could be shown no mercy, especially if it meant compromising his own safety. Being at war was such a horrible way to spend one's time.

The group quickly searched the wreckage. Hans shot three wounded horses to silence their agonised death throes because he found their distress utterly ghastly. He told one of the Frenchmen to release the other horses. They were trapped in their harnesses but were otherwise unhurt. As soon as they were free, they galloped off across a neighbouring field.

A cursory search of the scene yielded a couple of weapons, a few loaves of rye bread, some sausages, a case of beer, six packs of cigarettes, three undamaged jerry cans of petrol, two small medical equipment kits, a Wehrmacht Leica 35-millimetre camera and some singed bedding. The Frenchmen squabbled over the camera so Hans dropped it in the road and stamped on it to shut them up.

The group started off again as dusk fell. After about half an hour, they sought refuge in a copse of trees set back from the road. Hans drew up a guard duty rota but the Frenchmen were not keen on it and Hans made up his mind to leave them at the first opportunity. He still couldn't work out why they'd been so against him shooting the guard. War was a nasty business. For Hans, survival depended on ruthlessness and decisiveness. They should have appreciated him for saving their lives, not resented him for killing the German.

They eventually settled down for the night after a good supper of the German victuals. Hans then made a show of falling asleep while he waited for first light to make his move. Everyone was still asleep, including the guard on duty, so he sloped off into the woodland before turning back onto his compass bearing from the day before. He abandoned the German jacket, forage cap and Schmiesser machine pistol but took the Walther P38, the binoculars, a loaf of rye bread, a large salami sausage and an oval German army water bottle. He felt a huge sense of relief at having left the motley and undisciplined group of Frenchmen behind.

Hans hiked on all morning, his breath visible in the crisp air. He heard plenty of aircraft and distant gunfire and he was forced to take cover several times as low-flying fighters hurtled overhead. He was now extremely pleased with the way his Austrian hiking boots were performing. They were being thoroughly tested over the rough terrain but they were holding up well.

At noon he changed course to bring him back on bearing. After an hour or so the woodland thinned out and he emerged into open country. The lack of cover worried him so he searched for a thicket and made himself snug. He then snatched a welcome nap after eating some salami and rye bread and taking on water.

He woke a little later and gathered his belongings. There

wasn't much military activity in the vicinity but the distant sounds of warfare kept him on his toes. After a few hours he came across a temporary airstrip. It was quiet now but the ranks of smouldering French Morane-Saulnier MS406 aircraft hinted at recent action. He checked them over to see if any were serviceable but they had been totally destroyed by enemy fighters. He had been having visions about breaking through the German lines and hotfooting it across the Channel to safety.

Hans found it strange that the aircraft had not been properly spread around the field. They'd been left in formation like sitting ducks. Such stupidity did not say much for the fighting qualities of the French air force. He entered what looked like the wrecked control tent but it had been looted. Finding nothing of interest, he headed for the road opposite. It was streaming with civilian refugees so he hiked parallel with the road until he was in open countryside once more.

He eventually stumbled through a hedge onto a small road that just about followed his bearing. He was feeling the pace now and decided to have a rest. He found a plantation of young pines close to the road that gave good cover and made a mat from pine fronds. The smell of fresh pine seemed to act soporifically and he soon drifted off to sleep.

A sudden noise alerted him and he was wide awake in a flash. He crawled towards the road and found a German eating his lunch next to his motorcycle and sidecar. He had an Organisation Todt armband.

Hans pulled out his P38. "Stand up!" he barked.

The German almost jumped out of his skin, but he whirled round and tried to draw his pistol in a lightning move.

"Don't do it!" Hans hissed. "I'm not afraid to use this."

The German noticed the steely glint in his eyes and the cruel twist to his mouth and wisely backed down. "I'm with a bridges and culvert clearing inspection unit," he said eventually.

"Have the French been leaving booby-traps for you?" Hans asked, the tension in his stomach tightening.

The German shook his head. "We've had very little to do. They must have retreated south so fast they didn't have time to mine anything."

"Take off your uniform and boots," Hans said firmly. "I won't harm you as long as you clear off as fast as you can."

"Can I take my greatcoat out of the sidecar?" the Todt man asked.

Hans thought for a moment before nodding. "You can also have your boots back."

As the German loped off down the road he turned and saluted. "Thank you, my friend. You English are not so bad after all."

After the events of the last few days, Hans didn't feel like giving the man grief. He knew it was stupid to let him go, but he wasn't in the mood for killing a young man who was simply clearing the roads.

Rummaging in the sidecar, he found a field radio, several tins of meat, some smoked salami and rye bread, and a container of water. He also discovered a theodalite with a folding tripod, a twenty-five-metre tape measure and a Mauser field rifle. Hans threw the surveying equipment into the bushes and checked how much petrol was in the tank. It was three quarters full.

He donned the jacket – with its Todt armband – the helmet and gloves, and stowed his rucksack and binoculars in the sidecar. The BMW started first time. Every so often he ran into German military traffic but to his relief he found that a Todt motorcyclist was almost invisible. Hans covered plenty of ground and drove well into the night. Eventually the motorcycle started to misfire as it was starved of fuel. As he passed some woodland he turned into the trees and the bike spluttered to a halt.

Hans had a quick bite to eat and fiddled with the high-quality field radio. He eventually picked up a BBC transmission and listened intently to the first news he had heard since leaving Belgium. Things sounded pretty bad. It was only May 28 but the Belgian army had already surrendered. British and French troops were being evacuated from the beaches along the coast near Dunkirk. He reckoned the seaside town was a little to the north of his present position. He briefly entertained the idea of finding a small boat somewhere on the coast and using it to cross the Channel but the plan was unrealistic. The Germans knew hundreds of thousands of troops would be trying the same thing and the coast would be well patrolled.

He tuned into some of the German radio channels. They were playing marching music and making sickening triumphalist announcements. He wondered if this Teutonic attitude had deep historic roots or was instilled in the German people by the grossly arrogant strutting of Kaiser Bill, who he knew to be completely different from his English and Russian cousins.

Hans busied himself breaking off a few pine branches and covering them with dried bracken for a bed. He then had a small snack before settling down for the night. The dawn chorus woke him at around five, and he was briefly confused about where he was.

The moment soon passed and he spent a few minutes opening one of the German tins of coarse pork pâté, which he ate with pieces of rye bread torn from the loaf. He relieved himself in the motorcycle's petrol tank, then stripped the ignition leads and threw them away. He then hid the uniform and helmet in a bush. He wished he could take the field radio with him but reluctantly buried it after removing and destroying the frequency crystals and valves.

The day was turning out fine and warm, which was typical for late May. Hans hiked for a couple of uneventful hours until he emerged from a line of bushes and came up against a chain link fence topped with barbed wire. The fence disappeared into the distance in both directions so he decided to breach it.

The fence had probably been designed to keep animals in but it was no good for keeping humans out. Putting the tip of his heavy knife into one of the links, Hans began to lever it out. With the loop straightened, it was simply a matter of unthreading the thick wire down to where he could step through the V-shaped opening.

After climbing through the fence, he threaded the wire back in place so as not to make it too obvious that someone had broken through. He then lay in the long grass, watching and waiting for half an hour. No sentries appeared so he made his way stealthily across the grass apron towards the silhouette of distant buildings.

It was obvious now that this was another abandoned airfield. The first building he reached was a hangar with its doors hanging off at a drunken angle. He slipped inside, his nostrils assaulted by a mixture of pine timber, amyl acetate, glycol and 100-octane aviation fuel. He felt his way round one wall in the stygian blackness. He dare not strike a light with all the fumes so his progress was slow. He tripped and fell a couple of times and his heart stopped. But no one came, no searchlights shone, no alarm sounded.

He eventually arrived at an unlocked door, which he gingerly opened. A dim grey light filtered in from a row of windows opposite. He bumped into several empty packing cases. He checked one and found it full of fresh-smelling wood wool. He made himself comfortable in the soft material and, using his rucksack as a pillow, was soon fast asleep.

Hans woke in the grey light of dawn to find the room crammed with opened packing cases. After peeing in the corner, he crept back into the hangar and out of the wrecked door. The control buildings opposite seemed largely intact although they had been raked with small-arms fire.

Everywhere was deserted and there was debris all over the place that made progress difficult. Nothing seemed to be locked. It was getting lighter all the time so he decided to familiarise himself with his environment. His priorities were to find food and water. Entering what appeared to be a deserted office, he rifled through the desk and found a solitary Callard & Bowser toffee. This told him it must have been a British airfield.

Hans then froze in shock as something was poked into the small of his back. "Don't shoot, comrade," he said in German.

"Christ! A bloody Hun!" a voice exclaimed. "Turn around slowly and stand against the wall with your hands in the air. Any tricks and I'll shoot."

Hans did as he was told and saw a nervous RAF corporal wielding a Lee Enfield .303 rifle. "I thought you were German," he said in English.

The corporal's face registered blank astonishment. "Who the hell are you?" he barked eventually.

"I'm a Danish pilot trying to get to England," Hans replied.

The slightly built corporal with his youthful looks and unkempt brown hair motioned Hans through an adjacent door into a small and sparse room. Placing a chair against a wall he sat his prisoner down before sitting opposite. "Have you got any papers?"

Hans carefully took out his passport and slid it across the floor to the corporal.

The corporal gripped his rifle between his knees and examined the passport carefully, his emerald green eyes absorbing every detail. "How do I know I can trust you? I can see this is a Danish passport, but that doesn't tell me much. Where are your military papers?"

Hans shrugged. "I don't have any military papers." He quickly explained how the war had caught up with him. "I am not with the military, corporal. I was an engineering officer and pilot. And the truth of the matter is this: if I was your enemy, you would be dead by now."

"How come?" the corporal asked as he snapped back to full alert and snatched up the rifle.

Hans slowly stood and turned, then carefully took the Walther P38 from his belt and slid it across the floor. "Be careful," he said. "It is loaded so keep your finger off the trigger."

The corporal poked the weapon gingerly with his foot. "Point taken. You could have shot me as soon as I put the rifle down. It's not even loaded because I can't find any ammo for it. Take your pistol back," he said. "I don't know anything about automatic pistols and have never fired one."

"What are you doing here?" Hans asked as he slipped the pistol back into his belt.

"I was left as a rearguard with two other airmen," the corporal explained. "I was trained in demolition. We were supposed to destroy the remaining stores and abandoned aircraft but we thought that might attract the attention of the Hun. My mates left a couple of days ago in a Bedford truck to buy provisions but they never returned."

"I'm sorry to be the bearer of bad news," Hans said quietly, "but they were captured by the Germans and killed during an air attack."

"How do you know that?" the corporal asked.

"I rescued the Frenchmen who survived the attack," Hans replied. "It looks like you're on your own. Would they have talked?"

The corporal shrugged. "I doubt it, but you never know."

"If they did," Hans explained, "and the Germans passed the information on before they were killed, it's only a matter of time before their colleagues come looking for you."

"I've seen the odd vehicle pull up at the main gate," the

corporal said. "But they haven't bothered to come in.

"Is the place booby-trapped?" Hans asked.

The corporal shook his head and led Hans outside. "We had no time to lay our charges. As soon as all the serviceable aircraft left for Blighty, the place was abandoned except for us poor sods."

The airfield was littered with wrecked and burnt out aircraft, fuel and water bowsers, various trashed vehicles, the remains of ground-support equipment and plenty of other detritus. Hans noticed several wrecked Hurricanes but one in particular caught his eye. It had one undercarriage wheel and a bare oleo leg so it stood at a forlorn angle. The cockpit canopy was open and the wings and fuselage were full of gaping holes.

"Are any of these aircraft serviceable?" Hans asked.

"Not a chance," the young corporal replied. "They've been stripped by our riggers of anything useful: guns, magazines, radios, pitot tubes, air speed indicators, compasses, bank and turn indicators, altimeters, clocks and most of the other instruments. In some cases they even took the engines, dinghies and wheels – Uncle Tom Cobley and all. There are a few new tyres for tail wheels in a storeroom but no main wheels. All the parachutes have gone, except for a few damaged ones."

"What about fuel?" Hans asked.

The corporal led him to a sandbagged depression behind the main building. There was a stack of corrugated cardboard boxes bearing the yellow Shell Oil logo. Each box doubled as the protective covering for a shiny four-gallon tin of petrol. The rectangular tins had a small loop handle on the top but no opening, just round swaged caps in opposite corners.

"How the devil do you get the petrol out?" Hans asked.

"It's quite easy," the corporal explained. "You use a screwdriver to bash a hole in the cap and lever it off. You then make another hole in the other cap to let the air in otherwise it won't pour properly."

Hans couldn't quite believe their bizarre method of storing fuel. "They must have been designed by a committee," he said with a straight face.

The corporal didn't seem to get his joke. "I doubt it."

Hans still couldn't understand why the cans were so different from the ones used by the Danes, but, with plenty of fuel available, a plan slowly formed in his mind. He wasn't sure whether he could rely on the corporal for help but he seemed an intelligent sort. "What did you do before joining the Royal Air Force?"

"I was a carpenter and joiner and scene rigger on the film sets at Shepperton studios, sir," the corporal replied. "My employer was retained by the Ministry of Information but, along with several fit and able-bodied blokes, I was released to join the forces."

Hans pointed to the wrecked Hurricanes. "I happen to know quite a bit about these aircraft. The Finnish air force bought twelve of them and one of the Hawker delivery pilots landed in Copenhagen to let the Danish air force have a look. I actually sat in the cockpit and recommended that we buy them but the government wasn't interested."

The corporal nodded. "87 Squadron had both Mark 1s and Mark 2s but only these Mark 1s were abandoned. You can tell them apart because the Mark 1s were fitted with a two-bladed wooden propeller and had fabric-covered wings."

Hans walked over to the one aircraft that looked like it might fly again. It was shielded from the rest of the airfield by piles of burnt out wreckage so hadn't been completely destroyed. The others were missing propellers, engines and wheels but this one was in comparatively good condition.

"See if you can find hand tools and serviceable ground support equipment," he said to the corporal. "I also need spare fabric to make patches for the holes and dope to use as an adhesive."

Hans watched him disappear into a hangar before climbing onto the wing. He leaned into the cockpit but it was an absolute mess. Nearly all of the instruments, including the boost gauge and bank and turn indicators, had been removed. But the seat was still in place, as was the control column and emergency hydraulic pump arm. The canopy and fittings were also intact. The radio had gone but the engine and main battery remained, as did the 24-volt generator and all the wiring.

He jumped down and followed the young Brit inside. "Corporal, what's your name? I can't keep calling you by your rank."

"I'm Tony," the corporal replied. "My real name's Evelyn but that sounds a bit too poncey, especially now I'm in the mob."

"Okay, Tony," Hans said. "You can stop calling me 'sir'. My name is Hans but, as that is a German name, you must call me Ned."

Tony had no objection, but he couldn't help wondering why a Dane would want to be called Ned. "Does that come with an explanation?" he asked.

Hans smiled for the first time in ages. "One of my best mates at the English school in Copenhagen was a boy called Dennis but we knew him as Den. I got lumbered with Ned because it was Den backwards. We were inseparable so it was always Den and Ned. I don't remember who came up with the idea but it stuck and I became Ned at school. All my relatives hated it for some reason."

"Ned it is then," said Tony.

Hans started separating the important bits and pieces from the detritus. "We'll need to evaluate everything if this mission is to be successful. Now, I don't know about you but I'm starving. We should eat before we start."

"Follow me," Tony said with a wink. He led Hans into a smaller store where there were hundreds of emergency ration packs. Some were intact but most had been pilfered. "Grab a few of the undamaged ones and I'll show you where the water is."

In yet another small storeroom, medical supplies were stacked from floor to ceiling along with bottles of distilled water. Next door was a clothing store. Hans decided to kit himself out with a new RAF uniform to lessen the risk of being shot if captured. He found a pilot officer's tunic complete with wings, which must have been somebody's dry cleaning that hadn't been collected. He even found a new peaked hat that fitted perfectly.

Tony had rigged up an effective charcoal heater in the office. He fanned it to life with a homemade bellows. "It would be a bloody sight easier if we had electricity," he grumbled. "There are plenty of new batteries and bottles of electrolyte but nothing to keep them charged with. I'll have to build the brazier because I can't find any sand with which to make a sand and petrol cooker."

He put a container of water on the brazier and waited for it to boil. Then he tipped in several packets of the tea/dried milk/sugar mixture from the ration packs. He saved the Horlicks tablets in the flat tins and chocolate from the packs for later. The dry-tack biscuits were quite good covered with Marmite, of which there were plenty of tins.

Hans found the American tinned meat known as Spam beyond horrible except when it was fried. He grimaced as he watched Tony tucking into the uncooked processed meat with apparent gusto. How he longed for the German salami sausage and rye bread he'd left behind. Although they could get boring if eaten all the time, if there was nothing else on the menu, salami and rye bread were substantial and filling foods. Spam, on the other hand, was abhorrent.

While the two men ate, Hans outlined his plan. "We've got to repair that Hurricane, Tony. We'll use our engineering skills to overcome the problems grounding her. We'll strip absolutely everything that we don't need for flying."

The way Hans was explaining it made it sound ridiculously easy but Tony wasn't so sure and he raised a barrage of objections. "It's too far gone, Hans," he moaned. "You'll never get her onto the runway, let alone into the air."

Hans suddenly realised why Tony was being so negative. He obviously didn't like the idea of letting a foreigner fly off to his homeland leaving him behind. "You'll be coming along as my passenger, Tony. All the deadweight we're stripping from the aircraft weighs much more than you because you're quite small."

"Where the hell am I going to sit?" Tony blurted.

"In the cockpit under the seat pan where the pilot's parachute would normally be stowed," Hans replied. He wolfed down another lump of Spam and almost vomited. He knew he had to keep his strength up, however, so he fought to keep it down. He waved his hand over all the debris littering the ground. "You'll have to make me a seat using parts from these old chairs. It'll need central support legs to help distribute my weight."

"You've overlooked two things," Tony said flatly. "We can't get the old girl airborne on one wheel and there are no parachutes."

Hans smiled and gripped his shoulder. "You're going to build a light but sturdy trolley that fits over the wheel-less oleo leg and runs on two small tail wheels on either side, a bit like large furniture castors. This contraption will be loosely fitted so it drops off when we get airborne."

"How are you going to land?" Tony asked uneasily.

"We'll have no option but to do a wheels-up landing on grass when we arrive," Hans replied. "Parachutes will be useless because we'll be flying far too low for them to open." He grabbed a pencil from the floor and found a scrap of paper to write on. "You'll have to find the timber to build the trolley and seat. We also need nails, screws and parachute cord to fasten everything together. Make the holes you need using a red-hot steel rod because we've no drill or drill bits."

Hans took a gulp of water and checked that Tony was taking everything in. "I'll get to work on the engine. I'll have to remove the double-stage supercharger because there are no boost control components. This will make the Rolls-Royce Merlin a normally aspirated engine. I'll run a diagnostic check on the twin-bladed propeller, cooling systems and controls, and the wires to the control surfaces. I'll then have to insulate the bare electrical wires and terminals that used to connect the stripped-out instruments, as well as checking the hydraulics and operating gear."

"Is that all?" Tony asked facetiously.

Hans gave him a stern look and put him in his place. "The hydraulics, engine oil and glycol levels will have to be checked for leaks, and then I'll service the line filters. I'll also have to find a battery trolley and enough live batteries to start the engine. And that's what worries me. We are in a race against time, Tony. We have to work out how to charge up the battery packs. Please give this some thought while you work."

"Perhaps we can find a working petrol engine amongst the abandoned ground equipment and couple a 24-volt aircraft generator to it," Tony suggested.

Hans nodded slowly. "You know what, Tony," he said quietly, "we might make a flight engineer of you yet."

Hans watched him glow with pride and get stuck into his work with more determination than ever. He needed no supervising and Hans was impressed with his fabric-patching skills. He was pleased that they were making progress because they could not work in the dark.

A couple of hours later, while they were having a quick but well-deserved tea break, Hans heard a vehicle approaching. He glanced out of one of the front windows and saw, to his consternation, a Kuebelwagen (the German equivalent of Willy's Jeep), its two occupants slowly surveying the airstrip's perimeter.

Hans swiftly pulled on some brown dungarees to hide his uniform. The jeep eventually pulled up outside their building and the driver switched off the engine. Motioning Tony to stay where he was, Hans walked swiftly outside and said loudly in German: "Thank heavens you got our message and made it here in time. I have twenty RAF prisoners who need relocating to our camp at –" As he broke off, Hans brandished the Walther P38. "Put your hands up now!" he barked.

Unfortunately, the passenger made as if to escape. Hans was about to shoot him in the leg to disable him when Tony rushed over and smacked the German on the head with the butt of his .303 rifle. He misjudged the ferocity of his attack, however, and inadvertently killed the German. Poor Tony was then violently sick at what he had done.

Shaking like a leaf, he mumbled, "I've never killed anyone."

The trembling driver still had his hands in the air. "Coward!" he hissed.

"Get some parachute cord, Tony," Hans said firmly.

A visibly shaken Tony bound the driver securely by the elbows to avoid stopping his circulation. He then pushed the German into the back seat of the vehicle.

Hans, as ever, was one step ahead of the game. "We can use the jeep to solve our problems," he announced proudly. "I was worried that we wouldn't be able to tow the Hurricane to the end of the runway but now we can manage that and charge the batteries."

They dragged the body of the passenger into the building and covered him with a layer of parachute silk. They then searched the jeep and were delighted to find more German rations. The enemy soldiers certainly weren't lacking in supplies. There was fresh water, a bottle of schnapps, a half-case of Beck's beer, a box of fifty black Brazilian cigars, a flare pistol in a neat aluminium attaché-style case with a selection of four coloured flares, and the usual salami sausage and rye bread. The jeep toolbox contained some useful tools, including a set of hexagonal socket wrenches, which Tony called Allen keys.

They worked with greater urgency as the German patrol would undoubtedly be missed at some point. They removed the wheel faring from the wheel-less side of the plane to allow the trolley to slide freely onto the oleo leg. It was difficult to remove the retaining nuts without spanners, and they had to be loosened with a centre punch and hammer which was quite time-consuming.

Hans checked the jeep's tool kit and, despite the box of spanners being metric, found one that was a near-perfect fit. This speeded them up no end. He then uncovered a damaged but working engine hoist that he could rig to lift the aircraft. He cushioned the wing with wads of parachute silk and a small dinghy and just managed to get the oleo leg high enough to slip the trolley underneath. Another few centimetres and it wouldn't have been possible.

It looked a terrible lash-up but it was fairly lightweight so he was convinced it would work. They were able to charge the 24-volt aircraft batteries by running a cable from the 12-volt generator on the jeep. It was pretty straightforward to divide the battery plate terminals into 12-volt units for charging before connecting them up in series as 24-volt blocks. Hans decided to charge at the maximum rate even though he knew this would wreck the batteries by throwing deposits into each cell. He wasn't too bothered because they were only going to be used once.

The Hurricane's fuel tanks were empty but they didn't have any leaks. It took ages to fill them using the stupid four-gallon tins and they were spilling as much fuel as they poured in when Tony spotted a large tin-plate filter-cum-funnel which made the job much easier. The filter was doubly useful because it meant the fuel would not get contaminated.

Hans had removed the line filters from the engine fuel system to avoid misfires or a fatal engine stoppage if they became blocked. A bit of muck wouldn't do the engine any good but it shouldn't wreck it. Their last job was to plait together a substantial towrope from parachute cord to tow the aircraft and starter trolley to the far end of the runway. They found a towrope in the jeep but it didn't look strong enough so they hitched it up to pull the battery trolley. When they were finally done, it was dark on their second day.

They slept fitfully that night and were wide awake before dawn. The terrified German was still sitting in the back seat of the jeep. Feeling sorry for him, Hans popped a Brazilian cigar in his lips, lit it for him and wished him good luck.

In the first light of dawn, they crept out of the hangar. They left a row of spiked oil and petrol containers in front of the buildings and then towed the Hurricane to the end of the runway as quietly as possible. As a few streaks of sunlight appeared over the woods in the east, they climbed into the cockpit.

Tony slipped the bolt out of his rifle and dropped it in his top pocket. Then he threw the weapon onto the grass.

"What are you doing?" Hans asked.

"It's our policy never to leave our weapons behind," Tony explained. "But for some reason they only count the bolt as the weapon. I'm only obeying orders."

"If we're attacked," Hans said, closing his eyes and shaking his head at this ridiculous rule, "we don't stand a chance. We've no parachutes or dinghy."

Tony crouched on the floor and curled up under the seat but he was clearly in considerable discomfort. "Death would be a blessing over this," he muttered. "And I can't see my .303 being much help. It wouldn't even fit in the cockpit."

Hans ignored him. He was in his element now and was all

67

business. "You'll have to use the emergency hydraulic pump handle to help operate the landing gear when we're airborne."

Tony nodded and grabbed the handle.

The big question in Hans's mind was whether the engine would start. After turning over for what seemed like ages, the engine suddenly roared to life, streaks of flame and smoke bursting from the exhausts up front. Hans clenched his fist in triumph and took a deep breath. There was no ground crew, of course, to disconnect the starter cables, but the initial forward speed did the trick and they came clear. With the canopy still open, Hans fired a flare at the hangar's silhouette as the Hurricane trundled past. The initial flash soon turned into a huge blaze as the fuel cans went up.

CHAPTER 5

Running the Channel

The taxi run before take-off seemed to go on interminably, probably due to the reduced power from the Merlin engine. The end of the runway was fast approaching when Hans at last felt the aircraft get lighter. He eased the control column back and the Hurricane lifted off cleanly and quite suddenly into the crisp morning air.

He noticed that there was a worrying drift to starboard. Apart from this, Hans also found the Hurricane was poorly trimmed and he had to correct it immediately. The drift was obviously being caused by the disparity of drag between the bare oleo leg and the leg with the wheel and faring.

He and Tony pumped hard to augment the hydraulics and they quickly retracted the undercarriage. This almost corrected the drag, although a little drift remained due to the missing faring. Hans was able to hold his course and the aircraft seemed to fly reasonably well. He pulled up in a shallow climb until he saw a faint glimmer of light reflecting from the English Channel. He made a small course correction as they crossed a line of chalk cliffs on the French coast and then he brought them down to about twenty metres above the water for the first leg of their crossing. During their escape, not a single shot appeared to have been fired at the Hurricane.

A short while later, Hans pulled the nose up into a steady climb. Without an airspeed indicator, he had to guess his speed from the engine's revolutions. After flying for around twenty minutes, he reckoned they were at about fifteen hundred metres at two hundred miles an hour. The sky seemed to be empty, although the Channel below was dotted with small vessels trailing distinctive wakes.

Hans soon got a welcome glimpse of the hazy English coastline on the horizon and he brought the Hurricane down low above the waves. Flying this close to the water it was easy to misjudge your height and smack into a swell and he was forced to fly by the seat of his pants, which ate up fuel. The cockpit reverberated with the engine noise reflected back from the water's surface and the din made even thinking difficult.

As they approached the coastline, he found it much easier to judge their height. He throttled back a touch and crossed the coast near the town of Hastings with Dungeness promontory slightly off to starboard. He climbed again to get his bearings and was pleased to see welcoming swathes of green countryside stretching out beneath them. He started looking for a smooth grass field in which to land but there were too many woods for comfort.

The last recognisable landmark Hans noticed was Bodiam Castle, which the Hurricane roared over with only a few metres to spare. He saw a meadow on his right and brought them round with a deft nudge on the control column and left rudder. His heart was in his mouth at the prospect of deliberately crashing the beautiful aircraft but they had no choice and touched down in the direction of Tunbridge Wells.

The rear fuselage hit the ground first. The Hurricane immediately tipped forward and the propeller whipped the grass on the soft turf. The vibration was absolutely horrific and it felt as if the bones would be shaken out of their bodies. The juddering then subsided as the wooden propeller splintered into a thousand pieces. Without its drag, the engine screamed in protest and immediately seized. They then bounced along in comparative silence. The high-speed slide seemed to go on forever so Hans decided to open the cockpit canopy.

They were heading for a line of oak trees and a thick hedgerow but fortunately they slid to a stop a few metres short. Aside from the warm ticking as the aeroplane cooled down, there was a total and eerie silence. Hans struggled out of the cockpit and onto the wing. He then turned and removed his seat to give Tony a hand but he noted with consternation that Tony appeared lifeless, his head leaning over to one side.

For a terrible moment he thought Tony was dead. Hans shook his shoulders and breathed a sigh of relief when he finally came round. He must have fainted from the buffeting on landing. Both airmen were bruised and shaken but otherwise unhurt. After hugging each other in relief, they sat on the wing for a few minutes to recover. Hans found it strange sitting so close to the ground. A chorus of English songbirds mixed with the smell of hot metal and freshly crushed grass.

Hans almost blacked out with relief as the adrenalin rush subsided. "Welcome home, Tony," he said eventually.

"Are we really in Blighty?" Tony asked. "I couldn't see a bloody thing from the time we took off until we crash-landed."

"Landed will do, thanks," Hans said with a mischievous grin. He grabbed his rucksack and his new uniform. "Come on, my man, this is where you take over."

Tony checked that the bolt of his .303 rifle was still in his top pocket and threw a linen bag full of hundreds of tins of Horlicks tablets, which he had insisted on bringing along, over one shoulder. "I'm afraid I have no idea what to do," he said at last.

Hans shook his head in mock exasperation. "Must I do everything?" he grumbled good-naturedly. "There's a road up ahead. Let's hitch a lift into Tunbridge Wells in case it has a railway station."

They gingerly started out in the direction Hans indicated but they'd hardly covered any ground when a couple of breathless middle-aged men rounded the end of the hedge.

"Where is the poor devil in that Spitfire?" one of them asked. "Did you see if he made it?"

"It was a Hurricane," Hans replied. "And I'm not dead."

The man gave a bewildered shrug and turned to Tony. "You got him out then?"

Tony shook his head. "Actually, he got me out. We came over together."

Muttering something that sounded like 'Fisking knitters', the men ran off in the direction of the downed Hurricane.

Hans and Tony walked along the deserted lane behind the hedge for about half a mile until they came across a roadside pub called The Red Lion. It was far too early for it to be open, but they heard tuneless whistling coming from the open door of the public bar. All the chairs had been put on the tables and the bar stools were upside down on the bar. A big hairy man in his sixties, with his braces tied round his ample waist as a makeshift belt, was mopping the floor.

"Do you mind if I use the telephone to ring for a taxi to Tunbridge Wells?" Hans asked politely.

"No need for that," the cleaner said. "You won't get a taxi at this time of the morning but if you go round the side you'll find Fletcher the drayman offloading some barrels. He's off to Tunbridge after this drop so you might want to hitch a lift with him."

They slipped round to the cellar and asked Fletcher the same question.

The drayman had no objections so Hans gave him a hand lifting an 18-gallon barrel onto the stillage. "I'll have to spile the barrel and drop in some finings so you'll have to wait a minute," he explained. "Maurice, the landlord, is in the army reserve and he's been called up. Poor old Purkiss here has been press-ganged into running the place pro-tem but he hasn't got a clue. It's not his fault so I help him as much as I can."

Fletcher nodded to Purkiss when the stand-in manager

appeared at the side door. "These kind chaps are buying me a pint for my trouble."

"That newly stillaged barrel won't be ready for hours, mate," Purkiss replied. "Why don't you order three pints of light and mild instead?"

Hans nodded and paid for the round with one of the liberated five pound notes. "This should cover it."

Purkiss gave the note a disapproving look. "It only comes to one and ninepence. Haven't you got change?"

Hans shook his head. "I'm afraid not."

A grumbling Purkiss asked him to sign the back of the note before disappearing inside.

Hans had forgotten how big the English coins were, as well as the ragged state of their pound and ten-shilling notes. He guessed that such antiquated coinage must wreak havoc on the nation's pocket linings but decided not to mention it. He sipped from his beer instead. It was warm and sweet but still quite refreshing.

When they finished their drinks, they jumped on the brewer's dray and settled back to enjoy the ride into town, and they eventually arrived in Tunbridge Wells.

Tony had given up on getting any sleep. "I need to report to the nearest police station so I can return to my squadron."

Hans nodded slowly and held out his hand. "Our flight would not have been possible without you, Tony. I'm extremely grateful for your help." While Fletcher had his back turned, he handed Tony a wad of five-pound notes. "Do not tell anyone where you got these," he whispered.

Tony pocketed the notes and returned Hans's firm grip. "Thank you for everything. I'll never forget what you did for me."

Having thanked Fletcher, Hans set off towards the station so he could catch a train to London to report to the Danish authorities. It was only sometime later that he realised he had not given Tony his home address in Copenhagen, and he had no idea of Tony's address here.

He put the disappointment to one side and found a little junk shop. He bought a battered suitcase for his rucksack, uniform, hat and tunic. He soon discovered that, unlike in Europe, the English behaved as if they were at war. Most people carried gasmasks, including the children. Crossed bands of brown paper protected every pane of glass in the windows. And there were people in uniform from the navy, army, air force and civil defence everywhere. The big difference with Germany was the number of girls in uniform.

Danish men considered English women to be a bit plain, flat of chest and prone to wearing tweeds and flat shoes. Hans discovered to his delight that nothing could be further from the truth. Most were pretty and vivacious, and had good figures. They did not seem the least bit shy in their fetching peaked uniform hats. Hans realised with relief that his adventure had done nothing to lower his interest in the opposite sex, despite the pounding his parts had taken during the crossing and landing. But thoughts of returning to Louise stopped him from getting carried away.

Another contrast between Germany and England was the almost universal use of horses on the continent. Although he saw the occasional horse and cart here, there were many more trucks and even the occasional steam lorry. And the showing of papers seemed low priority compared with Germany. He eventually arrived at London's Victoria Station after only having to show his train ticket.

The drab and blackened vista filled with slate-roofed little tenements was quite depressing, but he marvelled at the contrast with the imposing Victorian architecture of the station. It seemed much bigger, indeed greater, than he remembered. He tried to compare it with Copenhagen Central Station. Here there was the assault on the ears, the shunting of steam engines, the blowing of whistles and the shouting of the porters, and they all coalesced into what felt like a typical English cacophony.

He left his suitcase at the left luggage for the maximum period, bought a brown envelope at a stationery shop, and posted the left-luggage ticket poste restante to the Victoria post office. He went to all this trouble because he did not want to carry the microfilm, all the five-pound notes and his Walther P38 and ammunition around London, let alone the German sausage.

The thought of using the London Underground filled him with foreboding and he also ruled out catching a bus, a form of transport he'd thoroughly disliked before his experiences in Belgium, probably because of the superior Danish trams and the S-train system in Copenhagen.

He waited patiently for a taxi and learned it was the norm for fares to share if they were going in the same direction. He ended up sharing with an elderly and somewhat pompous little officer who had a large wart on the side of his nose and was swinging a swagger stick as if he owned the car. The taxi driver called him 'brigadier'.

Sitting there in silence, which he found embarrassing, Hans tried to lighten the moment. "Tell me, Brigadier, are you enjoying some leave?"

The brigadier pointed dramatically to a poster on the cab partition, which read: Careless Talk Costs Lives.

Hans felt as if he'd been brought down to earth with a bump. The brigadier arrived at his destination shortly before Hans and dug in his pocket as if intending to pay.

Hans held up his hand. "I'll get the fare."

The brigadier turned on his heel and walked off in his heavy overcoat, a quick lift of his swagger stick conveying his thanks. At least he gave him the benefit of the doubt.

"The brigadier is a regular fare," the cabbie said. "He's been brought out of retirement and is in charge of a battery of anti-aircraft guns in Hyde Park."

So much for secrecy, Hans thought. When they arrived, he paid the driver and was given another handful of enormous coins in change for his pound note. He assumed it was normal to give a tip so Hans gave the man one of the large silver coins, which he learned later was a half crown. He got the impression from the driver's face that he had given him far too much and realised he had a lot to learn if he wanted to blend in.

Hans noticed that most of the entrances to the buildings lining the streets were heavily sandbagged, and some were guarded by soldiers standing at ease. He arrived at the right address but either he'd written it down wrongly in his pocket diary or the office had moved because the metal sign at the entrance said: Ministry of Strategic Materials Procurement, South.

It looked as if the engraved sign had been there for some time. Hans felt he'd reached a dead end. He decided to get some refreshment and use the time to plan his next move. He walked for a little while before he came across a small café with taped up windows.

He approached the counter and looked in vain for a menu. "I'll have a cup of coffee with sliced salami on rye bread, please," he said eventually.

"A cup of tea and a bloater paste sandwich is all you'll get here, mate," said the assistant. "That'll be sixpence."

Hans handed over one of the small silver coins he had in his pocket. He'd tried tea on his previous visit to England but did not remember it being this weak, milky or sugary. Nevertheless, he found it curiously invigorating, and he was offered a second cup at no extra charge. The sandwich had a trace of margarine and some fish paste and was quite unpleasant. Despite being hungry, he could only manage a mouthful.

He didn't know anyone in London but thought about trying to find the Danish Club, which had been established in the eighteenth century and was where he had lunched on a previous visit. After finishing his tea, he walked back to Victoria, absentmindedly window shopping on the way. He walked on into Pimlico to look for somewhere to stay the night. He knocked on the door to a guesthouse but there was no answer. He tried several more but had no luck. It was only then that he noticed the streets were almost deserted.

He crossed the road and approached a man with bulging eyes and a tartan waistcoat who was walking a tiny dog. "Excuse me, sir," he said politely. "Where has everyone gone?"

"There's a big Gerry raid coming in," the man replied, "and they are all in the shelters. The ack-ack guns in the park haven't opened up yet so the raid will probably start shortly."

"Why aren't you in a shelter?" Hans asked.

"I've got a phobia about those places," the man explained as they arrived at his flat. "I'd rather die here with the mutt than be cooped up down there. Will you come in and wait for the all clear?"

Hans nodded his thanks and followed the man inside.

Over a cup of extremely strong tea in the man's attractive book-lined study, he explained how the air raid warning and all clear were sounded and they soon heard the long single note signalling the raid had passed.

Hans eventually thanked the man for the tea and retraced his steps. He tried another two places but still couldn't get anyone to answer their doors. It was only when he turned from the second door that he noticed two men in gabardine raincoats and trilby hats waiting for him on the pavement. Hans felt a shiver run up his spine. One of the men had a thin, angular face and beady eyes that seemed to be able to bore right through him. With his hooked nose he reminded Hans of an eagle about to strike at its defenceless prey. The other man was short and squat and looked like he ate bricks for breakfast.

They clearly meant business.

CHAPTER 6

Big trouble

The man on the left smiled thinly, revealing a set of even white teeth. "May we see your pay-book, please?"

Hans shrugged. "I don't have one. Will my passport do?"

The man studied the document. "You are clearly of military age but for some reason you can't produce your pay-book. Please come with us."

Hans followed them to an Austin Six saloon a little way up the street and was ushered into the back seat. One of the men slid in next to him and they drove to Victoria police station. Hans was shown into an interrogation room and offered some tea. It arrived with two arrowroot biscuits. The authorities here were clearly much more civilized than the Gestapo in Aachen, Hans mused.

After a while, two men came in and sat down opposite. They couldn't have looked more different. One was tall and thin with pale skin and tiny eyes, the other short and muscular with a distinct redness to his nose that hinted at a problem with alcohol.

Shorty examined his passport in detail. "Where do you come from?" he asked eventually.

"My passport tells you I am from Denmark," Hans replied evenly.

"And you were born in Bellahøj, Copenhagen?"

"That's what my passport says," Hans said with an impatient sigh. He knew they were playing games with him so he let them know he was wise to their tactics.

78

"That may be so," the interrogator said quietly. "You tell us you are from Denmark, yet your friend Mörz is from Holland."

Hans had no idea who Mörz was or what they were talking about so he said nothing.

The taller man fixed him with an icy stare and leaned forward until Hans could smell his breath. "You must have known we'd find it strange that you didn't understand how our air raid warnings worked."

Hans realised that the man who'd given him tea must have notified them. "What did he tell you about me?"

The shorter officer nodded slowly. "He was quite clear that you spoke English with a faint German accent."

Hans decided to tell them his story so he explained how he'd escaped from Germany (although he omitted mention of the gun sight drawings), re-engineered the Hurricane, flown to England with the RAF corporal, and that it was his burning desire to join the forces fighting Hitler. Even as he spoke he could tell they were not buying it. He had to admit that it all sounded like a boys' adventure story and he'd have had a hard time believing it too.

The men listened with detached amusement.

"The Hurricane is a single-seat fighter so your story simply doesn't wash," the taller man said with a healthy dose of cynicism. "Despite the fact that you're obviously telling us absolute nonsense, we'll try to corroborate your bizarre claim. However, it'd be much better for you if you explained when you were going to meet Mörz, and where you've hidden your transmitter, code books, revolver and money."

Hans felt a prickle of fear run down his spine. Things were not going as he'd expected, far from it in fact. If he couldn't make them believe his story, there was a good chance he'd be shot as a German spy.

"Who can vouch for your identity?" the shorter man asked coldly.

"I don't know anybody living in England," Hans replied. "But if you find the corporal he'll confirm my story. I couldn't contact the Danish authorities so I was looking for lodgings when you grabbed me."

"It's quite clear that you were going to your contact's address," the wiry detective said smugly. "We know you were with a second person but we've yet to trace him. You people never come over alone. Give me your contact's address and your operational instructions and I will put in a good word for you. Otherwise your future looks bleak."

Hans lifted his hands, shrugged and ran a hand through his wavy hair. "I have no contact address," he said emphatically but with a hint of desperation because he had no idea what they were talking about. "You must have me confused with someone else."

"We don't make mistakes," the taller officer said with a sharp exhalation. "It is my duty to inform you that you are being detained under the aliens act. You will spend the night in our cells and be transferred to a detention centre tomorrow where you will be subjected to a full and exhaustive interrogation."

Hans was shown to a sparse cell with a bolted-down bunk, two coarse blankets and a zinc bucket. He was later given a meal with some bread and butter and the obligatory mug of strong tea through an opening in the door. He was under the impression that prisoners lived on bread and water so he was quite pleased with the way he was treated. He soon learned that the Geneva Convention required prisoners to be given the same rations as the military. He seriously doubted the Germans adhered to the same policy.

The officer who collected his tray handed him a well-thumbed copy of the Canadian *Reader's Digest Magazine*, which Hans knew from Denmark as *Det Bedste*. "Lights go out at ten," the officer stated abruptly. "They won't come on again until five in the morning."

As they had taken his watch and the cell had no windows,

Hans had no idea what time it was. He thought he might be in a mild state of shock after the events of the day. He was eventually plunged into darkness so he felt his way to bed without undressing and dozed for a bit. He woke up when the lights suddenly came on in the middle of the night. He was told he was on suicide watch and the light would remain on until the morning.

Despite the light, he managed to get a full night's sleep, which was unusual for him, although he didn't feel particularly refreshed in the morning. He was given a mug of tea at about half past five, and at half past six he was handed a traditional English breakfast of egg, bacon, fried tomatoes and toast with more tea. Regrettably, coffee did not seem to be available in England.

At about ten in the morning, Hans was handcuffed and taken to a car with blacked-out windows. It was nice to breathe fresh air, even if it was only for a short time. He had no idea where he was being taken but he hoped he would not have to face some kind of trial before being shot. He was not blindfolded, which was a surprise.

The car soon left London and its never-ending suburbs, and drove for about two hours into the countryside, which, he guessed, took them out towards Cambridge. He was ignored for the entire journey. The car eventually pulled up at a pair of black wrought-iron gates that were guarded by four surly officers. The driver and his escort left Hans and entered a small guardroom. Hans thought about making a run for it but that would only imply guilt and the guards looked trained to shoot at the first sign of trouble.

His escorts returned a few minutes later and the car continued up a long drive through attractive parkland to the imposing front entrance of an extremely large house. Hans was led inside and body-searched for the umpteenth time. A uniformed officer of medium height and build, with short dark hair and a day's worth of stubble, and who was all business, then entered the room. He held the door open for the escort and driver and they disappeared. Hans was motioned to chair at a large table, on which lay his Danish passport and wallet.

The officer spoke impeccable German with a slight Hamburg accent. "You will be kept here while we check your background and find out why you've come to England. You will not be imprisoned within this building, and will be free to associate with your fellow prisoners. You will be interrogated every day. Have you anything to say?"

"I find it odd that even though you know I'm Danish," Hans said in English, "you persist in speaking to me in German."

The officer's eyes narrowed and he looked like an animal about to pounce. "I'm convinced that you are a highly trained German agent who is part of an Abwehr cell that has entered the UK to carry out acts of sabotage preceding an invasion under the codename Operation Sea Lion. You are being held in a facility where only German is spoken. You speak with barely any accent, which hints at your German roots. The penalty for such activity is death, but if you cooperate there's a chance you won't be hanged. Your colleague, Mörz, has finally been apprehended. He was masquerading as a Dutchman and now we have you pretending to be Danish. Tomorrow you will be interrogated by two Danish officers to see if they can verify your story."

The officer stood and waved him to the door. "You are now free to leave. Turn left and you will find the common room through the first door on the right. You will be shown to your sleeping quarters later."

Hans ignored his circumstances for a moment and marvelled at the beautifully appointed house. The doors were all solid Honduras mahogany, the rooms hung with oil paintings, fine porcelain abounded, and plush oriental rugs covered the floors. Hans found the right door and entered the common room. It was large and well lit by French windows that opened into the park.

It was furnished as he imagined an exclusive English club might be. Men were dotted about in black leather easy chairs. Some were sitting at tables playing chess or the card game Skat.

He guessed there were perhaps forty men in the room. Some wore Wehrmacht uniforms, others their Luftwaffe clothing, and a sprinkling wore black SS uniforms. A handful were in civilian clothes like Hans, his RAF uniform having been confiscated. He was astonished to note that there were late editions of German and Austrian newspapers available, as well as *The Times* and *The Daily Telegraph*.

"So, you are the new boy, eh?" a voice said.

Hans turned to find a tall German approaching, his hand extended in greeting. "Apparently so," he replied.

"Heinrich Kaltenberg," the German said with a curt nod. "I was captured or, more accurately, kidnapped four months ago in Norway."

"Hans Gundelach," Hans replied. "I'm a Danish citizen who was arrested in London yesterday."

Kaltenberg raised an eyebrow and beckoned Hans to follow him out onto a vast lawn dotted with marble sculptures. There were evergreen yew bushes around the perimeter, through which the high metal fence with coiled barbed wire ringing the top could be seen.

Hans noticed the evenly spaced porcelain insulators that told him the fence was electrified. Even at this distance he could hear a low crackling hiss that told him the voltage was extremely high. There didn't appear to be much chance of escape.

When Kaltenberg was reasonably sure they couldn't be overheard, he leaned forward with his hand covering his mouth. "It is important you keep up your story because the house is brimming with hidden microphones. Spools of these recordings are sent away every day for analysis. There are a number of stool pigeons in our midst but don't ask me how I know that. We are also monitored by lip readers using binoculars. In the next few days, you will be approached by a trusted officer who will be on the staff of Kaltenbrunner. After playing Skat with him you will be pressured to socialise. You were expected and your capture is a serious setback. Your new friend will debrief you during your walks in the grounds. You must try to maintain your cover but the British are fiendishly clever at penetrating the best stories so you'll need a lot of luck. Heil Hitler."

Hans found the way he flapped his hand during the salute quite comical. "I'll bear that in mind," he replied quietly.

Later that afternoon, Hans was shown his sleeping quarters by a German orderly. He was allocated a bunk in an airy dormitory with four beds. They had individual bedside cabinets and wardrobes. The dormitory also had a table and four chairs in its centre. One of his fellow bunkmates was sitting at the table reading a book. The orderly left and the two men introduced themselves.

"The English treat their prisoners humanely and there have been no violent interrogations so far," Herr Erling explained. "Occasionally they let us know that someone has buckled under pressure. If they're found guilty of espionage, they're executed by hanging. This is rare but it angers us inmates."

Hans couldn't help noticing that morale was sky high, which indicated to him that there was a high proportion of diehard Nazis amongst the prisoners. He suspected that because the Germans were winning the war, good morale was to be expected.

They were given a light supper at nine o'clock and the lights went out at eleven. Hans slept quite well given the circumstances. The next morning he was taken to an interrogation room on the second floor. He sat on his own at a table for about ten minutes before two men briskly entered the room and closed the door.

"Sorry we're late," said one in businesslike Danish. "There was an air raid in London this morning. Now, please outline your family background, schools, university and friends."

Hans's career in the Danish air force, his boyhood visits to Aachen, his impeccable German and good English were then exhaustively examined.

After nearly three hours, a British intelligence officer joined them. "Two lines of enquiry will now be followed up," he explained. "The Danish exile community in England will be canvassed for anyone who knows the Gundelach family, and enquiries will also be made in Denmark. The occupation of the country is still in its early stages and no reliable underground links have been established. Any information will have to come out via Sweden or Danish consular officials in Switzerland, and this will take time to verify."

Then, surprisingly for Hans, they all had lunch together. The conversation, now in English, turned to Danish food. Hans was careful about what he said because he felt that lunch was part of his psychological evaluation. This was his routine for a number of days and he began to relax, but he immediately realised that might be a mistake because they were bound to notice any change in his behaviour. It was odd that he occasionally felt pressure to admit guilt, even though he'd done nothing wrong. He steeled his defences against the clever ruses designed to break him down. He somehow had to get them to believe his story. He thought about mentioning the suitcase again but it was a double-edged sword. They might see the microfilm drawings and money as proof that he was a spy. The cash and gun had been taken from a German officer and were probably standard issue for agents of espionage.

When he entered the common room one day he was asked by a strikingly handsome, blue-eyed Prussian officer with the obligatory duelling scar if he would like a game of Skat.

Hans realised immediately this was his supposed Abwehr contact. He nodded and sat at the table.

The shaven-headed man introduced himself as Ernst von

Klauber. "If the weather is good tomorrow, we should take some exercise in the park," the officer said, his tone of voice telling Hans that this was an order rather than a suggestion.

Hans nodded again. Although there was something about Klauber he didn't like, he couldn't put his finger on it but his instincts warned him to tread carefully. He decided to play along with the German in the hope that he'd find out some useful information to give to the British. (He didn't find out until much later that Special Branch had installed long-range listening devices on the roof of the house and were able to eavesdrop on conversations anywhere in the park! Hans didn't realise, therefore, that his good intentions could perhaps be helping to dig his own grave...)

The next day he walked around the park with Klauber as they'd planned. Initially, their conversation revolved around general topics such as the progress of the war, but the officer gradually brought them round to the real purpose of their meeting.

"There's a rumour going round that after intense interrogation most of the men who pass the vetting process are sent to a prisoner-of-war camp in Canada," Klauber said.

Hans didn't reply because he sensed there was more information to come.

"Stand still," the German said suddenly. "I want to whisper something in your ear." He leaned closer and cupped his hands. "Remember what I have to say and do not commit anything to paper. If you get out of here, contact Hans Jaeger at 21, Anson Road, Tufnell Park, London. He is an important contact and will instruct you on what to do next, but you will need answers to his questions if you are to convince him you are the genuine article." Klauber then whispered the code-words in his ear. "If your interrogators ask what I'm doing," he added, "you will tell them that this was a homosexual approach and that you rejected me. Understood?"

Hans nodded and the pair continued their walk back to the house in silence. Sure enough, the next day during interrogation Hans was told one of the guards had seen Klauber whispering in Hans's ear.

Hans didn't know whether to tell them what had actually happened or what Klauber had told him to say. He wanted the British to trust him, which should mean telling the truth, but he wasn't sure exactly where he stood. "I'd rather not say as it's an upsetting personal matter," he said eventually, feigning embarrassment.

"Try," said the interrogator.

Hans took a deep breath and finally admitted that Klauber had made an improper homosexual proposition to him. "I rejected him as I'm not of that persuasion," Hans added.

He was not pressed further on the matter, but he noticed that Klauber was nowhere to be seen the following day. He hoped it was the last he'd see of the slimy officer. A couple of days later, Hans was told to get ready to transfer to a different facility. After breakfast, his living area and body were searched before he was handcuffed to a burly escort and taken out to a dark green Austin Six. They soon left the house and began the long drive back to Kingston-upon-Thames on the outskirts of London.

"Where are you taking me?" Hans asked.

"Camp 020 at Ham," the driver replied flatly.

They eventually pulled up at pair of sturdy gates topped with barbed wire just off the road running past Richmond Golf Club. Hans couldn't believe it. He'd once been a guest of the Danish Ambassador and they'd played a round or two and had lunch here. He vaguely remembered that the course had been good but quite worn, and the lunch pretty awful. A pair of guards waved them through and the car stopped outside a single door in a sprawling line of buildings in grounds. The buildings were surrounded by a substantial wooden fence, inside which were two double barbed-wire fences.

Hans was told he was one of the first people to arrive at Camp 020. It was now July 28. He was taken to a guardhouse manned by uniformed military police and was then ushered through three more security checks, which seemed a little excessive. His personal details were recorded at the final security check and he was then taken to a room for yet another body search, which included having a particularly unpleasant enema. Afterwards, he was shown into an alcove and blindfolded while ultra violet lights carefully examined his skin. He was taken from here into another room where he was given a pair of brown dungarees. He was then photographed in his prison clothes as well as a set of civilian clothes before being locked in a good-sized cell. After a couple of hours, he was escorted to an office.

A stern-faced officer with a monocle sat opposite. "I'm Lt Col Stephens," he said, standing.

Hans nodded curtly as Stephens sat down. He could tell that this was a man you didn't cross. Although his brown hair was slicked back and his monocle gave him a slightly comical appearance, there was a hardness about his middle-aged body and his face oozed unnecessary brutality. "Hans Gundelach," he replied.

"You have been brought to Latchmere House because we suspect you were part of Operation LENA," Stephens began, his tone sharp and official. "While we find out what your role was, you will be treated humanely and in strict accordance with the Geneva Convention. You will find, however, that your new home is considerably tougher than what you've been used to. You have been asked to cooperate but have so far refused. If your complicity in LENA is established, you will be shot in accordance with the Geneva Convention. Have you anything to say?"

"Yes I do, colonel," Hans replied evenly, fixing him with a barely disguised look of contempt. "I'm a little surprised that you still haven't established my identity when you must have discovered by now that my Danish passport is genuine."

"It is of little value to establish the validity of someone's passport," the colonel said, ignoring his challenge. "Central Danish passport records are now under German control and no lists exist outside Denmark. I run a tight ship here. We will eventually prise the truth from you and that experience will not be pleasant. However, I give you my word that we will not resort to physical torture."

Hans now realised how spoiled he had been thus far. "You haven't accepted the truth yet," he said softly. "So I've little faith you'll change your minds and believe my story now."

Stephens appeared to absorb what he'd said, then nodded towards the door. "I'll see you in the morning."

Hans slept fitfully on a metal bed that pinged and creaked whenever he moved, which was often as he found it difficult to get comfortable. He couldn't help thinking about this Mörz character and his contacts. He wondered if he'd really been caught or if that was just another trick to get Hans to confess.

In the morning he was escorted to a sizeable room and made to stand in front of a large group of people. A pair of serious WAAF stenographers sat at tables on his right. Hans was thoroughly cross-examined in English, the questions fired rapidly at him by various people. He wasn't given a break and after several hours he returned to his cell shaking with fatigue and nervous exhaustion. He realised how difficult it would be for people with something to hide to survive such a protracted ordeal.

The food at Latchmere House was based on standard army rations but the staple ingredients were comprehensively murdered by the 'chef' in the kitchen. As he was among the first intake, he assumed that the kitchen staff had not got used to catering for such numbers but, as time went on and the food failed to improve, he assumed it was all part of the method of breaking agents down. This assumption turned out to be false: the English, it seemed, had no concept or interest in quality cuisine.

Hans eventually settled into a daily routine comprising two periods of intense questioning that examined both his life and the extraordinary events that had overtaken him since he'd left Denmark. The questioning was repetitive and he grew tired of playing the game of cat and mouse with his interrogators. Every night he would try to drift of to sleep but it became harder with each day spent away from Louise. He'd initially been afraid that not seeing her for months would harden his heart but the opposite was happening: each day his feelings for her actually intensified and he longed to return to her.

One dreary morning during yet another session, an orderly brought his interrogator tea and biscuits. Hans was only offered water in a chipped enamelled mug. His *Eureka!* moment came suddenly and unexpectedly. As he was eyeing up the biscuits on the tray, he noticed they were lit by a dapple of sunlight streaming in through the window. He read the embossed lettering on one of the biscuits: English Arrowroot. He suddenly leaped to his feet and banged the desk with his fist. Of course! English! The little English boy!

CHAPTER 7

A change of fortune

Hans was ordered to sit down by a guard standing behind him.

Hans did as he was told but there was hope mushrooming inside him. "There is someone who can vouch for my identity in England," he said breathlessly. "I know a mother and her two boys. If they made it home before Denmark was occupied, they'll confirm my story."

"Where do they live?" the interrogator asked.

Hans shrugged. "I don't have an exact address but one of the boys told me he lived near his grandfather who was the blacksmith in a village called Abinger Hammer in Surrey. Their family name is Potter."

The officer leaned closer, his eyes narrowing. "Why didn't you mention this before?"

"It slipped my mind under all this pressure," Hans replied. "I was only thinking of my friends and relatives."

The interrogating officer huffed and left the room for some time. The guard standing behind Hans made him feel uncomfortable and he was glad when the officer returned.

The officer leaned across the desk. "Enquiries will be made based on the information you've just given us so I hope you're not wasting our time."

If Hans thought his release was imminent, he was sorely mistaken. He was harshly interrogated for another couple of days, by which time he was mentally and physically exhausted. One morning the following week, when he thought he could take no more, he was taken to a different room. There was a stenographer, several easy chairs and a Danish interrogation officer.

He sat in silence for nearly half an hour before the door opened and there, exactly as he remembered him from Holstebro all those weeks ago, was the little English boy and his mother, Aase. The reunion brought a lump to Hans's throat. The boy had grown a couple of centimetres but the youthful twinkle in his eyes showed how pleased he was to see Hans.

He came over and shook Hans's hand in a very grown-up way, and he then talked twenty to the dozen.

When he eventually paused for breath, the officer asked him to be quiet for a moment and turned to his mother. "Do you know Hans Gundelach?" he asked firmly.

Aase nodded, her smile infectious. "I know his family very well," she replied in Danish. "He is a pilot in the Danish air force. My father is a great friend of his uncle. I often chat with them when Hans here entertains my sons with his flying stories. I can give you details of several Danes here in England who know the family, but who Hans personally might not have met."

Hans smiled as he recalled the times they'd spent together. "How did you get back to England, Aase?"

"The boys and I embarked on a small Norwegian ship, the *Dronning Maud* (*Queen Maud*), at Esjberg in Jutland," she replied. "After a long and rough crossing she berthed at the Pool of London. The ship then returned to Norway but she was sunk by German aircraft in the North Sea."

"And all the bottles in the bar sank to the bottom," the little English boy said.

"When he found out she'd been sunk, he burst into tears," Aase explained. "I quickly told him that all the crew had survived, but it was all the soda pop going to the bottom that had brought on the tears."

After his initial burst of Jutland patois, which had probably been brought on by excitement and which completely confused the translator, Hans tried to talk to the boy in Danish, but he always answered in English.

"He's refused to speak Danish from the day we arrived back in England," Aase said. "I think that he enjoyed his school days in Holstebro so much that he resented being sent to a school over here. I can only hope he accepts his English school someday soon." She looked down and ruffled his hair with her hands and noticed from the look on the interrogator's face that the meeting was over. "Goodbye, Hans," she said with a thin smile. "Please get in touch when you leave here."

Hans was sad to see them go, especially the little boy. He crouched down and gave him a fatherly hug and then shook his hand once more.

It was several days before Hans's routine changed as the family had to be thoroughly vetted by the Secret Intelligence Service. He was soon dragged to a final interview with Lt Col Stephens.

The officer nodded politely and offered him a chair. "What will you do when you're released?"

Hans rubbed the stubble on his chin and stared out of the window. He'd noticed that he'd aged in the last few weeks. The youthful adult who'd looked back at him from the mirror had acquired lines of worry on his forehead and his first few grey hairs. "I'd like to join one of the allied fighter squadrons so that I can help avenge the invasion of Denmark," he replied. "At the end of hostilities, I'd like to play a part in rebuilding the Danish air force."

Stephens shook his head and frowned. "Joining a squadron could take some time and you're bound to have to undergo a familiarisation program on whichever aircraft are in service. In the meantime, the Danish authorities have arranged temporary accommodation in London for you." The lieutenant colonel paused as if embarrassed about what he had to say. "I'm not allowed to apologise for your treatment because that would mean apologising for doing our job." Then, in what seemed like an uncharacteristic flash of humour, he said, "I can, however, apologise for the God-awful food. You'll be glad to hear that we have to endure it as well! Anyway, good luck for the future, Gundelach." He shook hands quickly but firmly before disappearing with a flash of his monocle.

Hans had his self-issued RAF uniform confiscated so he was left with the rather nondescript jacket and trousers he'd been given at the magnificent house near Cambridge. He was escorted to the front of the building and a car took him to an address in Clanricarde Gardens in London. A Danish consular official was waiting for him, and he was reunited with his Danish passport.

"Your arrival in the UK has been clandestinely forwarded to your parents," the official explained, "but the good news could take months to get there via Sweden." He then showed Hans a pleasant one-room first-floor flat and handed him a wallet with cash for general living expenses. He also gave him a grey ration book and a red clothing book with extra emergency coupons. "Be patient, Hans," he said, holding out one hand and opening the door with the other. "Someone will contact you."

The first thing Hans did was run a hot bath to wash away the odour of his incarceration. He lay back in the cast-iron tub and almost dozed off on a number of occasions. He eventually climbed out and towelled himself dry. He couldn't help feeling that the turn of events marked a watershed in his life. This was a new beginning so he decided to collect his suitcase from Victoria and go on a shopping spree. It was a luxury being able to do this of his own free will. It was all part of the new and strange environment.

Hans had to register with the local suppliers before he could buy any rationed goods. He bought basics such as sugar, tea, butter and a loaf of bread baked with national flour, which imparted an unappetising grey colour to the loaf, but which he found toasted quite well under the gas grill. Using the ration books had novelty value but it soon wore off.

He was told by one shop assistant that he'd bought his month's ration of sugar in one go.

"How much is that ration?" he asked with raised eyebrows.

"One pound," the assistant replied.

"In weight or money?" Hans asked, the peculiar system of weights and measures in England being somewhat confusing.

The assistant laughed. "Weight."

Hans had never been served coffee while he'd been imprisoned so it came of something of a surprise to find that it wasn't even rationed, and the beans were quite good quality. They were only sold in delicatessens where one bought the whole beans and then had them roasted and ground, which was an extraordinarily long-winded procedure.

He soon found an ironmonger and bought an airtight jar for the ground coffee and a bread knife. He needed more underwear so he bought six pairs of underpants, six string vests and a dozen cotton handkerchiefs. He offered the red clothing coupon book but was told these items were 'off the ration' but he could bring the book in if he wanted shirts, jackets or pairs of trousers.

He tried to buy a bottle of snaps but the owner of the sparsely stocked off-licence looked at him in bemusement. Whisky was not rationed but it was only sold to the 'regulars'. He would have to forgo his pre-war treat of a small glass of spirits at bedtime until he became a regular.

Back at the flat he disposed of his old underwear in a laundry bag and made himself a wonderful cup of coffee. He'd tried to buy a coffee pot in the ironmongers but the elderly assistant thought he must have arrived from another planet. Hans had also failed to find any milk. He learned later that it was delivered to one's door in pint- or half-pint bottles, or loose by the jug, by a milkman who arrived early each morning on a pony-drawn float.

He then emptied the contents of his rucksack on the bed. He checked the Walther and put it to one side, then counted the cash. He still had plenty of the five pound notes. But it was the microfilm that drew his attention. He still wasn't sure if he could approach the authorities with the drawings. They were so sensitive that he could quite easily be taken back in for questioning about where he'd got them. He decided to wait to be contacted before bringing it up in conversation. He prised a floorboard loose in the bathroom and slipped the microfilm underneath.

There were several public houses within a short walk but each one was quite different in character. He found that the ambience depended on the landlord's disposition and the class of the clientele. His favourite was The Green Man, which was run by a late-middle-aged landlady who was known to everyone as Mrs Witherspoon. A strict disciplinarian, she appeared to run the pub with a rod of iron and ensured it was always spotless. The regulars were mainly retired business people. During the winter months, Mrs Witherspoon always had a blazing fire.

Hans heard the occasional air-raid siren but they were usually ignored. It became part of his routine to drop in at The Green Man for three or four pints every evening. He was eventually allowed the odd shot of Glenmorangie single malt whisky. He considered this a great honour because it was in such short supply. Mrs Witherspoon obviously had a good network of contacts and she seemed to take to him, although he couldn't explain why.

As the weeks went by, there was still no sign of *his* supposed contact and he began to contemplate handing the microfilm over anyway. It was the height of the Battle of Britain and the country was still short on supplies because the U-boats were sinking an enormous number of ships in the Atlantic convoys. If he handed the drawings to the authorities, they might be able to devise a better way of detecting the submarines. He felt as if he was being forced into the decision but it was not to be taken lightly. He thought about running his idea past a few Danes living in London but few were his age or class and most would have no clue as to what should be done.

Several weeks after moving to Clanricarde Gardens, Hans was alone one evening in The Green Man reading a thin copy of the *Evening Standard* when a chap about his own age came in. He ordered a Light Ale and, to Hans's surprise, sat down at the same table.

"You're HG if I am not mistaken," the stranger said immediately in a low voice, his deep brown eyes appraising Hans from head to foot with a well-practised glance.

His intonation led Hans to believe he was a Londoner. "Who are you?" he asked quietly.

"My real name is inconsequential but you can call me Stanley," the man replied. "You don't know me but I'm sure you've heard of MI5. I am familiar with your case and have been assigned to monitor you. This is normally carried out clandestinely but as your case appears so special we decided the best approach was to be direct with you." He stopped and smiled to put Hans at ease. "Can we go somewhere and talk?"

Hans appreciated Stanley's apparent honesty. "Why don't you come back to my flat?"

On the way out, Hans studied Stanley a little more closely. The agent was of medium height but his worn and expensive dark grey suit couldn't hide his muscular frame. He wasn't wearing a hat and his dark hair was cut short in an American style. He had an expressionless and clean-shaven face – with a slight redness to his cheeks – clamped between two slightly protruding ears. Hans's initial impression was that he was the open and honest type, but he realised Stanley was probably quite adept at making people conclude whatever they liked about him.

The distant sounds of a raid wafted across the Thames and several searchlights pierced the night sky, their reflected light offering a welcome break from the blackout.

"The bastards are up there again tonight," Stanley hissed. "It's unforgivable to target the civilian population."

Hans nodded. "As a foreigner, I can't help admiring the courage of your people."

"The Jerries are not winning any brownie points using terror tactics," Stanley muttered. "The only solution is to do the same to them, but then I have a personal axe to grind."

"I'm not sure two wrongs make a right," Hans replied philosophically. "The general German population are good people but they have been betrayed by their leaders. It's up to us to bring those responsible to justice."

Stanley did not share his views but bit his tongue and didn't start an argument.

When they got back to the flat, Stanley, somewhat surprisingly, produced a half bottle of Bell's whisky from his jacket pocket. Hans fetched the only two tumblers he had, both of which were made from thick glass that had gone opaque over time. He placed them on the low table and Stanley poured a generous slug in each. They chinked glasses and sat back to enjoy the drink.

Stanley took a deep breath and came straight to the point. "Having been assigned to your case, I've listened to a number of boring aural intercepts and read your interrogation notes. With the exception of your Danish notes, I feel that I know you as well as you know yourself. But there is one thing I'd like you to clarify."

Hans sipped from his drink and savoured the warm liquid as it trickled down his throat and ignited in his stomach. "Fire away."

"When you were talking with the Abwehr creep, Klauber, in the park at Farm Hall in Godmanchester," Stanley said, "he leaned across and whispered something in your ear. This caused us some consternation at the time because you claimed, rather implausibly, that he'd made a homosexual advance. Klauber might have been a slug but he was definitely not a whoofter."

Hans hadn't heard the term 'whoofter' before but didn't need to ask what it meant. He was also growing to like Stanley. The intelligence officer was continuing to provide Hans with clues about his incarceration in an effort to build trust between them.

"Homosexuality is one of the key characteristics we look out for when assessing our prisoners," Stanley explained.

"Why did you use the past tense when talking about Klauber?" Hans asked suddenly.

"He's where he should have been years ago," Stanley said. "He was moved a few days after speaking to you but wouldn't admit to anything under further interrogation. As he had originally been arrested in civilian clothing, he was tried 'in camera' at Maidstone prison. After due process of law, he was found guilty of espionage and was hanged. He was invited to accept a pardon on the scaffold if he told us everything but he was a true Nazi fanatic and took his story with him to the grave. It might as well have been suicide. Now he's wrapped in quicklime, and good riddance, too."

Hans held out his glass for a drop more whisky. "He made me feel quite uneasy."

"Did he confide in you?"

"He gave me the name and address of a contact called Hans Jaeger," Hans replied.

Stanley raised an eyebrow in surprise and took a large swig of his whisky. "Why didn't you say anything?"

"Think about it," Hans explained. "If I'd mentioned this Jaeger, my fate would have been sealed. The Abwehr surely know their own people. Anyway, I'd decided to use the information to try to learn more about this German espionage nest."

"We believe that nest to be headed by a man called Mörz," Stanley said.

"I've heard that name before," Hans said. "Anyway, if I thought I was helping to destroy it, I'd earn some kudos and prove my loyalty."

Stanley nodded slowly. "You were put in a difficult situation."

"Which was made even more impossible when you tried to trick me into admitting something I knew nothing about."

"What do you mean?" Stanley asked, a deep frown creasing his forehead.

"Your agents told me Mörz had been captured."

Stanley leaned back in his chair and stared at the ceiling. "A barefaced lie to probe you for weakness," he admitted.

"So, who is the elusive Mörz?" Hans asked.

"I had assumed you knew," Stanley said. "I know differently now, of course. The security services and the police have been hunting Wilhelm Mörz for some time but they've got nowhere. We know he heads a German espionage ring here in England but we haven't been able to capture or identify anyone yet. Nor have we managed to turn anyone double agent, although we're working on a radio operator at the moment."

"When you caught me, you thought you'd made a breakthrough," Hans said quietly.

"You said it," Stanley muttered. "Mörz was originally a Hamburg police detective. He joined the Nazi party in January 1933 but earned a reputation for double-crossing informants. He penetrated anti-Nazi groups of German émigrés in Czechoslovakia and saw to it that hundreds were executed. He was also active in Holland, where he betrayed a number of Dutch anti-Nazis. He was even suspected of being the German agent responsible for carrying out the infamous Venlo Incident, where two British officers were snatched from inside Dutch territory."

Stanley poured himself another whisky before continuing. "We believed Mörz entered England in the guise of a Dutch refugee. His spoken Dutch was supposedly quite passable."

"Why did the Abwehr choose Mörz for the role in the first place?" Hans asked.

"Perhaps they were scraping the bottom of the barrel," Stanley suggested. "His spoken English is apparently not very good, but perhaps the Krauts thought we couldn't differentiate between a Dutch and a German accent."

"If that's true, they've made a big mistake," Hans said. "I know firsthand just how good the British are at sniffing out a foreigner."

Stanley nodded and sipped from his glass. "Mörz's main remit is to set up small but well-equipped sabotage groups that will cause confusion amongst the British when the Germans invade during Operation Sea Lion."

"If the Germans are planning on invading," Hans said quietly, "they'll have to be sure they control the air first. They can't risk exposing their ships and submarines to the RAF."

"The Battle of Britain is well underway," Stanley said. "At the moment the RAF is standing firm against waves of German fighters and bombers."

"If the British hold out, Mörz and his teams will be stranded in England," Hans said. "They must have a secondary objective should the air assault fail."

Stanley nodded slowly. Hans was clearly blessed with considerable insight but their conversation was about to enter a delicate phase. "The same thought had crossed our minds," he said quietly. "Our sources inside Germany repeatedly contact us with warnings about German agents trying to steal something called a cavity magnetron."

For once Hans was stumped. "I've never heard of it. What does it do?"

"I won't bore you with all the technical information," Stanley said, "but the magnetron is essentially a booster that enhances radar signals. It allows us to spot, and therefore track, German aircraft much earlier than before. We're also working on fitting portable prototypes to some of our aircraft."

"That could change the course of the war," Hans said quietly. "No wonder Mörz has been given the task of stealing it."

"If we can fit the device to our aircraft and not just have it powering the ground stations, we'll gain a huge advantage over the Luftwaffe," Stanley explained. "There's also the possibility that we could spot their submarines purely by their periscopes."

"If so," Hans said, "you could dispatch fighter bombers to intercept and sink them." He topped his glass up with another shot of whisky. "If the convoy losses can be reduced and the air war can be won, you'll give yourselves a fighting chance of staving off Sea Lion."

"Which brings us back to Mörz," Stanley added. "He's devilishly cunning but Special Branch has received sightings all over the country."

"How does he keep slipping through the net?" Hans asked.

"He operates through go-betweens who he's already manipulated," Stanley replied. "He's got great support and plenty of funding." He was coming to the crux of their conversation now and didn't know how Hans would react. "You were mistaken for his second in command, which begs the question as to whether you could get close to him."

"What happened to the real agent?" Hans asked.

"That's anyone's guess," Stanley said with a shrug of his powerful shoulders. "He's almost certainly dead, which we can't let Mörz know because it'll compromise your chances of taking his place."

Hans thought it a bit presumptuous to assume the agent was dead but, as he realised what was being asked of him, the line of enquiry took a backseat. The anticipation ran up his spine with a prickle of heat and he shifted his weight uncomfortably. "How on earth do you expect me to take down Mörz without any resources or back-up?"

Stanley smiled. "We traced you from the moment you got on the train."

Hans knew they were one step ahead of him so decided to come clean. "Then you know I brought a few things over from France."

Stanley shook his head. "We lost you in Victoria Station for a few minutes."

Hans appreciated his continued honesty and decided to reciprocate. "I stored a reasonably new Walther P38, two spare magazines and five or six boxes of nine-millimetre Parabellum ammunition in a left-luggage box at the station. I've also got several thousand pounds in five pound notes, a pair of Wehrmacht Ziess binoculars, some German army issue salami and a little rye bread."

Stanley whistled in astonishment and studied Hans's face for signs levity. "You're full of surprises. Where did all this come from and how come the Secret Intelligence Service doesn't know about it?"

Hans quickly outlined how he'd collected the bits and pieces while on the run in France, flown it into England and deposited everything in the left-luggage locker at the station. But he didn't mention that he'd already collected the rucksack. Although Stanley appeared honest, this was the first time they'd met.

Stanley couldn't hide his admiration. "What have you done with the key to the locker?"

"I posted it to myself and can collect it at any time from the post office at Victoria," Hans replied smugly. "I didn't think it prudent to travel around London with those things in wartime."

"You don't trust people," Stanley said.

"Danish military training teaches you who to trust," Hans said, "and how they should earn it."

"You're forcing me to make a big decision," Stanley said

eventually. "Do I pass on the information you have divulged, or do I suggest we tackle Mörz together unofficially? If we choose the latter and things go wrong, there will be the most unholy stink and my career will go down the pan. However, I have always been regarded as a bit of a maverick. Our security services have failed to deal with Mörz using conventional methods and all their resources, so perhaps the two of us can get a result. Are you are up for it?"

Hans shrugged but he could feel the anticipation rising in his stomach. "You'll have to give me a bit more than that."

Stanley thought for a moment and then nodded. "Until now, every spy caught on the mainland has been subjected to due process. Only one of them, Klauber, has been executed so far, so you can see how far outside the box we will have to venture. I can't legally pull the trigger, except in self defence, but you, as a foreign national, are not bound by the same laws."

Hans had thought of Stanley as a conventional person but here he was showing a different side to his character. He was assuming a more active role rather than playing things by the book. "When do we launch the operation?" Hans asked.

"The sooner the better," Stanley replied. "Almost everything we do will have to be un-attributable and, except in the most extreme circumstances, we will not be able to call for help."

Hans nodded. "Where are you based?"

"I have a private office suite in Acton," Stanley said. "It is secure and I have a combination safe." He scribbled the address on the blank 'late news' space in the *Evening Standard* and stood. "Get your stuff first thing tomorrow and take a cab over to the office. I will have to assess what you've got so for heaven's sake steer clear of the authorities. We'll then draw up a plan to scout for Jaeger in Tufnell Park." He glanced at the half-empty bottle. "You'd better put that away. We'll need our wits about us tomorrow."

Hans put the bottle in a sideboard. "There is one more thing,

Stanley."

The intelligence officer raised an eyebrow. "Why do I get the feeling you're about to drop a bombshell?"

Hans smiled thinly. "I had to be sure I could trust you."

"Trust me with what?"

"Before I escaped from Germany, I procured top-secret drawings for the latest U-boat deck gun," he said quietly.

Stanley's mouth dropped open. "You're just full of surprises," he said eventually. "You'd better bring them too."

CHAPTER 8

Business

Hans shook Stanley's hand and saw him out. Then he sat down and finished the whisky in his glass before cleaning his teeth and going to bed. He hoped that meeting Stanley and deciding to work together would bring results. As he was dropping off to sleep, he wondered whether the muffled sound in the distance came from the same raid or a new one.

His curiosity aroused, he climbed out of bed and opened the French windows onto a small balcony. He leaned out and listened to the incredible sound of hundreds of anti-aircraft guns firing at the German bombers. Beautiful flares lit up the night sky. Hans saw six or seven German aircraft amidst the shell bursts, their unsynchronized engines droning towards the Thames.

He wondered if the little brigadier was out there in the thick of it. The raid seemed to go on without let-up but it was nicely muffled when the balcony door was closed. Hans set a big brass alarm clock to wake him at six in the morning. It was the first time he had used it, so he hoped it would work. He was a habitual light sleeper so he wound an elastic band round the clapper so the noise didn't blast him out of bed.

The next morning he found it difficult to hail a cab but he eventually drew the attention of a loquacious driver who talked all the way and seemed to be the most opinionated person Hans had had the misfortune to meet. He didn't usually mind opinionated people as long as they were on the right track but this guy was in a league of his own.

Stanley's office was easy to find and occupied the entire ground floor of a small, poorly appointed and architecturally bereft row of drab Victorian buildings. Hans had to smile at the Verdigris-covered brass plate to the right of the front door that announced the proprietors as Stanley & Stanley Perquisites Ltd. Someone lifted the little brass cover on the inside of the door's spy hole, the tiny movement catching Hans's eye.

As he raised his hand to knock on the door, Stanley opened it with a flourish. "Come in, come in," he said amicably.

The tiny hall was furnished with a bentwood hat stand and a horrible elephant's foot umbrella stand that held several walking sticks and a broken golf club. Stanley showed him into his office, which consisted of one largish room furnished with two desks and a Chubb combination safe set into the back wall. There was a small kitchenette and stationery cupboard on the left and a lavatory out the back. The single window opened into a yard with a high creosoted wooden panel fence and some unfamiliar evergreen bushes.

Hans lifted his rucksack onto one of the desks and took out the Walther P38, the spare magazines and ammunition and the compact bundles of white five pound notes. He also took out a forty-centimetre length of German salami and pack of rye bread and tossed them into the bin. He then removed the Ziess binoculars.

Stanley examined the Walther P38 and realised it was almost new. He opened a box of nine-millimetre ammunition and whistled. "Did you know you had a box of explosive dumdums?" he asked, dropping a round into Hans's palm.

Hans saw the red marker ring for the first time. "I didn't check them closely, although I did flip the lids to make sure they weren't blanks."

Stanley exhaled slowly. "The officer you took them from must have been a SD executioner. These rounds are so effective that a headshot completely empties the skull. They are banned by the Geneva Convention and are thus illegal in the theatre of war. We never use them, even in non-attributable operations."

"What should I do with them?" Hans asked.

"Empty one of the full magazines and refill it with dumdum rounds," Stanley replied firmly. "We are going to need all our resources against Mörz. Now, let me see these suspect five pound notes."

Hans handed him samples from several packs. "I've used a few so if they're forgeries they must be good."

Stanley examined them for paper thickness, ink and watermark. Then he tested the black printing ink for water fastness. "They're definitely genuine," he said eventually. "We keep expecting German forgeries to turn up but none have surfaced so far."

"When I first saw them I didn't think they were real," Hans said, "because the backs of the notes are blank and they are printed on something resembling toilet paper."

Stanley laughed. "I know what you mean. They've never been popular and some smaller shops get you to sign the back, although I don't understand why." He nodded towards the waste bin. "What did you throw away?"

"Only the German salami and a pack of rye bread," Hans replied.

Stanley retrieved them from the basket and sealed them in a large brown envelope. "We have a department that examines enemy food. If it contains ten percent sawdust, we'll use it as propaganda."

Hans felt quite indignant, probably because the English sausages were so horrible. "I'm sorry to say that German sausages are of impeccable quality, Stanley. They have an excellent flavour and are a hundred percent pork, so they are also very filling. You can eat them cold sliced or fried with potatoes, and the rye bread never goes stale or mouldy."

"Sorry if I've touched a nerve," Stanley replied.

"They may be the enemy," Hans said philosophically, "but if they make something good, we should admit it. Take the Walther P38. It is standard issue in the Royal Danish Air Force and probably the best personal defence pistol ever made. It is also an excellent police and special services weapon. You can carry it loaded with the hammer down and then pull through on the trigger to fire the first shot. There are no wasted seconds fiddling with a safety catch. I was over the moon when I found it."

"I admit it is also a favourite of mine," Stanley conceded. "We have nothing here to hold a candle against it." He knelt by the safe, spun the numbers and pulled out a green P38. "It's a strange coincidence that we've got the same pistol. I'll have a few of those dumdums if you don't mind."

"Help yourself," said Hans. "A little treat courtesy of the Wehrmacht."

Stanley laughed and then looked at Hans in expectation. "I suppose you'd better let me see these technical drawings."

Hans removed the microfilm container and dropped it into his palm. "I'm afraid you can't just spread them out across the desk. I needed to travel light so insisted on taking them in microfilm form. We should get it to the authorities as soon as possible."

Stanley nodded. "If what you say is true, if this sight ever makes it onto the U-boats we'll be in big trouble. It'll halve the time they need to be on the surface, which will make it much harder for us to spot and sink them."

"This country is almost on its knees," Hans said softly. "If you surrender another advantage to the U-boats, the war could be over in a matter of months."

"That's why the German High Command is so worried about our countermeasures," Stanley said.

"You'll have to put that in your report," Hans said. "The top brass will need convincing."

Stanley carefully withdrew the two-foot spool of sixteen-millimetre microfilm from the aluminium cigar tube with a pair of tweezers and slipped it into an empty thirty-five-millimetre film container. Then he dropped the container in a concealed pocket inside his briefcase before throwing the cigar tube into the waste basket. "Considering where that's been, the bin is the best place for it! We'll drop the film off on the way to Tufnell Park. Do you know the place?"

Hans shook his head. "I've never been to that part of London."

"We should survey the area around the flat," Stanley said. "Only then can we plan our next move. You take Anson Road and meet me in Hangar Lane."

The two men drove into London and dropped the case off at Stanley's office, giving his colleagues strict instructions as to what should be done with the microfilm. They then headed out towards Tufnell Park. Anson Road was lined with semi-detached lodging houses. This part of London was quite far from the city centre and less liable to be targeted by the Luftwaffe. Stanley eventually pulled over to the kerb and let Hans out.

He walked up one side of the street, stopped at a small shop to buy a paper and then returned on the opposite side. He sat on a bench for a few minutes and made a show of reading the paper. His eyes took in every detail, his ears and other senses on full alert.

He eventually walked back the way he'd come and reported to Stanley. "Why don't I just knock on the door of Number 21 and ask for Mr Jaeger?"

"You'll be taking a big risk," Stanley warned. "Keep your pistol in the secret pouch sewn into the back of your trousers."

Hans was about to climb out of the car when, in typically English fashion, the heavens opened and the rain came down in great driving sheets for fifteen minutes.

"I'll drive you in closer so you're not soaked before you get there," Stanley said.

"Not too close that we arouse suspicion," Hans muttered.

Stanley drove to the end of Anson Road. "I'll be able to see you the whole time," he said reassuringly.

Hans smiled thinly and climbed out. It was still drizzling so he pulled his coat tight around his middle. He felt the tension rising in his stomach as he approached Number 21. He took a deep breath, swallowed in anticipation and used the knocker on the peeling white door. After a few moments it was opened by a rather attractive woman of about forty.

"Is Mr Jaeger home?" Hans asked.

"He's just popped out for some cigarettes," she replied, standing to one side and beckoning him in before following him into a Victorian-style lounge.

Hans could tell that the place was frequented by heavy smokers because it reeked; even the decor was covered with a brown hue.

"Please sit down," the woman said. "Can I make you a cup of tea?"

Hans politely held his hand up. "I've just had one, thanks." How often did he find himself using that phrase? All the steam seemed to have gone out of the operation but Hans guarded against the anti-climatic feeling. Although Jaeger's digs were not intimidating in the slightest, his heart was pounding in his chest and adrenalin was coursing through his veins. He was ready for action at a moment's notice.

Five minutes later the door opened and a tall, fair-haired, blue-eyed man entered. The woman, who turned out to be landlord's wife, made the introductions before disappearing into the kitchen. Jaeger invited Hans up to his room, shut the door behind him and asked him three coded questions.

He appeared satisfied with Hans's answers – thank God for

Klauber – and motioned him to a chair in the far corner. "We were expecting you a couple of months ago," Jaeger hissed. "This could jeopardise the entire operation."

Hans found his English slightly accented but his place of origin was indefinable. "It's a long and boring story," Hans said, handing him his passport.

Jaeger studied the document carefully. "They are getting very good. I can't tell that this is a forgery."

Hans was quietly amused that his genuine passport had passed Jaeger's scrutiny.

"The gentleman waiting for you has been desperately trying to find out what happened," Jaeger said. "It's put him under a tremendous workload." As he was talking he sat at a little desk and wrote something on a piece of paper. "Memorise this address, then destroy the paper. I will forward a message to your contact. You will be expected this Saturday. The password will be Tiger One."

Jaeger then stood and ushered him downstairs. "Good hunting, my friend," he said as he opened the front door.

Hans nodded curtly. He saw no sign of the woman and did not attempt to shake hands or say another word to Jaeger. He simply raised his hand in farewell and walked away until he was no longer visible from the house. He walked round the block once to make sure he wasn't being followed and soon found Stanley parked up in a side street.

Hans climbed into the car and handed him the address. "It looks like we're following a paper trail, Stanley."

"The agent read the address and shook his head. "We'll have to arrange RDF (radio direction finding) surveillance. I expect this property to be remote with no neighbours but we'll head down to Chessington to get a copy of the six-inch-to-the-mile ordnance survey map to make sure because it shows individual buildings. This information will be vital in assessing possible enemy escape routes and we can't leave any stone unturned in trying to capture Mörz."

"It's going to make for a long day," Hans muttered.

"We aren't nine-to-five operatives, Hans," Stanley countered. "We must take this bastard down. There is too much at stake."

Getting hold of the map involved cutting through a considerable swathe of red tape. When they finally got back to Acton, they pinned the map on the wall. Stanley produced a much smaller scale map of Sussex to show Hans exactly where they were on the large-scale map.

"The property stands alone on the chalk downs," Stanley said, "which means there won't be much in the way of cover."

"That's probably why they chose it," Hans said.

"Let's get down there and do a drive past," Stanley replied.

"By the time we get to Sussex it'll be dark," Hans said.

Stanley glanced at his watch and conceded he had a point so they agreed to start early the next morning. He made them a small late supper and they shared a few glasses of whisky before falling asleep on put-you-up beds in Stanley's office.

The next morning turned out to be bright and sunny and they made good time. The only traffic they met was military, apart from the odd bread van or milk float. The first thing they noticed about the house was that it was built at the base of a natural saucer-shaped depression in the chalk hills.

Stanley checked his compass and nodded slowly. "The terrain will funnel any radio transmissions coming from the property out across the English Channel. There'd be no frequency leakage inland, which would foil any RDF surveillance."

As they drove past, they could see that the property had a boundary fence and gates fronting the road. Much of the property was screened from the road by leylandi trees, but behind the occasional break they could tell the house had a white stucco façade and a slate roof. There was a summerhouse and a big shed in the garden. They drove on to the main coast road at Shoreham before turning left towards Brighton.

Stanley suddenly pointed at a faded sign and smiled. "See that gable with the advertisement for R.O.P. petrol? That's the cheapest pre-war petrol you could buy. It almost killed some cars."

"What does R.O.P. stand for?" Hans asked.

"Russian Oil Products," Stanley replied. "That's where we get our word 'ropey', meaning poor quality, from."

Hans shrugged because he'd never heard the word. "Where are we heading?"

"There are a number of estate agents along here," Stanley explained. "We need to find out if that property has been sold recently."

The pair struck gold on their third try.

Stanley told the agent that he was interested in buying the place and would retain him for any possible deal. The agent leafed through a cabinet and eventually found the relevant file. Stanley spread the papers across his desk. It transpired that the property had been left vacant for some time but had been sold in August 1939 to a Mr Keith Thomas. The exchange had been made with cash, which the agent found rather unusual.

Stanley swore the agent to secrecy. "I'll approach Mr Thomas myself," he explained. "If I can get him to deal, I'll arrange for your agency to retain a five percent commission."

The estate agent's eyes lit up as he held out his hand. "Consider that a deal," he purred.

Hans and Stanley then drove on to Portslade and had a meal in a fish and chip shop with steamed up windows. Hans had not eaten fish and chips before, but knew it was an English staple. For just one and three pence each, including tea, it was a cheap and curiously satisfying meal. He would have enjoyed washing it down with a bottle of cold lager but the sweet tea ran it a close second. Hans mentioned this and was surprised to learn that

114

Stanley had never heard of lager.

The SIS agent outlined their next move while they waited for their fish and chips to go down. "We'll have to split up again," he said. "You'll be compromised if they see you with me. The house is on a local bus route, so you can arrive by public transport. I'll observe from a suitably concealed vantage point."

"What do you want me to do if I get inside?" Hans asked, the nerves again tightening in his stomach.

"I feel guilty about putting a civilian in this position," Stanley said quietly. "Just find out as much as you can by saying as little as possible. If things get out of control, use your weapon and I'll be right there beside you."

Hans knew he was oversimplifying things. If he was discovered, he'd be executed on the spot. "Don't dally," he said eventually.

Hans had to wait quite a while for a bus to turn up. Thankfully it was much better than the Belgian bus he'd used all those weeks ago. There was no having to share with live chickens, only pensioners out shopping and a sprinkling of school children. There wasn't an official stop outside the target house but Hans asked the driver to pull over and he made no objection, especially when a ten shilling note found its way into his top pocket.

Hans glanced at the gates and noticed they were locked. He was wondering what to do next when he saw a button on the gatepost. He pressed it firmly but couldn't hear a bell. He thought it might be out of order but then he saw a Rottweiler running towards the gate. It was followed by a tough-looking man of about forty-five who had curly blonde hair, powder blue eyes and weather-beaten skin.

The man opened the gate and beckoned him through. "Don't worry about the dog," he said in perfect English. "He's a big softie."

"Is his name Tiger One?" Hans asked.

The man looked around to make sure they were alone. "Did you come in on the bus?" he asked in German with a Westfalian accent.

Hans nodded. "If I was being followed, I would have carried on."

"You did the right thing," the man said as he opened the front door into a large entrance hall with impressive oak staircase. He ushered Hans into a well-appointed reception room.

"You've a very impressive house," Hans said. "When was it built?"

"It belonged to the chairman of Martin's Bank and was built around the turn of the century," he replied. "Let me fetch some coffee."

Hans heard him talking with someone in the kitchen, which told him there was at least one more man in the house.

His host soon returned with a tray and set it on a long, low table. "Call me Peter. May I call you Hans?"

Hans nodded and sipped from his coffee. "This is lovely! You've no idea how much I miss good coffee when I'm over here."

Peter chuckled. "That is the general consensus, although there doesn't seem to be a shortage of quality beans, unlike in the Fatherland where there is talk of coffee rationing. We also can't find quality cigars. They have these tiny cheroots that they call cigars, and Havanas cost a fortune, but they don't have good everyday cigars like we have at home."

The men chatted for a few minutes about where they were from – Peter said he hailed from Wuppertal and Hans talked about Aachen – when they were interrupted by the mad barking of the Rottweiler and a buzzing from the intercom.

"Stay here, Franz," Peter shouted into the kitchen. "Hans, follow me!"

Hans followed him down a long, windowless corridor that ended in a large oak door. Peter led him into a brightly lit garage, where, to Hans's horror, they found a badly beaten Stanley. He was tightly bound to an old kitchen chair with fencing wire and was being guarded by a huge hulk of a man holding a First World War Luger.

"God in Heaven, Goeppert!" Peter bellowed in his strong accent. "Who have we got here?"

Goeppert shrugged his massive shoulders. "I was patrolling the beech grove when I nearly tripped over him. He refuses to talk but appears to be alone."

Peter turned and glared at Hans. "So much for not being followed. Do you recognise him?"

Hans knew he had to move fast. "I'm afraid so. He's been hanging around for some time and I was beginning to get suspicious." He turned to Stanley, his eyes narrowing in apparent anger. "How many of you are there?"

Stanley's only reply was a sullen stare.

Peter pulled his Walther from an underarm holster. "It looks like we've been compromised."

Hans's heart was beating like a sledgehammer now. He pulled out his own gun and levelled it at Stanley's forehead. "Let me do it. I have a score to settle with this bastard."

Stanley did his best to give him a look of abject betrayal but Hans knew he'd understood every word.

Hans motioned for Peter to stand aside. "You don't want to get splashed by an Englishman," he said as he squeezed the trigger.

"Do it now!" Peter hissed.

As the hammer was about to fall, Hans whirled and shot Peter in the chest with a dumdum round. Peter was still falling backwards when the monstrous Goeppert reacted. He was incredibly quick for such a big man.

Goeppert spun round and managed to get off a single shot. The muzzle flashed and the gun roared but the bullet narrowly missed Hans's face and embedded itself in the garage wall.

Time seemed to slow down for Hans and he had an age to plan his next shot and be certain of the kill. Goeppert took the round in the centre of his chest and slumped forwards in a heap. Hans immediately felt a pang of guilt and cursed the blasted war. What a filthy perversion it was.

The colour gradually returned to Stanley's face but he was clearly shaken and his breathing was short and sharp. "You frightened the life out of me. For one awful moment I thought I'd made a terrible mistake. Help me get this bloody wire off. It really hurts. That big bastard took me apart in unarmed combat and did me up like a kipper. Sorry to have let you down."

Hans helped him free himself but then remembered Franz. "Wait here, Stanley," he said as he rushed out of the garage. He charged back down the corridor and found Franz loading a shotgun in the living room. "Leave that," Hans barked. "We just shot a Special Branch officer and are probably compromised. Goeppert and Peter have been hit."

Franz looked absolutely terrified. "How bad is it?"

"I don't know yet," Hans replied. "I want you to get away as quickly as possible in case they're closing in. Make absolutely sure you are not followed." Hans was still thinking clearly and tried a long shot. "Where can I contact you when this blows over?"

Franz gave Hans an address in Beaconsfield Road, Brighton.

"Be careful," Hans said as Franz ran for the main entrance. "Only answer the door to me."

The Rottweiler was probably nervous about the gunfire but Hans found a beef roasting joint in the meat safe and it was soon occupied with its unexpected treat. He then went to the bathroom and found a first-aid box. He ran back to the garage and dropped the two automatics into a tray of sump oil in one corner. He then helped patch Stanley up as best he could.

He could tell the agent was still hurting and was afraid shock might set in so he bundled him into the living room and poured

118

them a couple of large whisky shots from a bottle in the sideboard.

Stanley held up his beautiful cut-glass tumbler. "Cheers, my friend," he gasped, his old self-confidence gradually returning. "I really needed this. Such a pity I had to leave that Luger. I've wanted one for my collection for ages but I suppose it would only remind me of the beating I took from Goeppert. Those German dumdums certainly retire people early."

Hans wondered if he was going into delayed shock with his ramblings. "I saw a Humber Super Snipe parked outside."

Stanley pointed over his shoulder. "The keys are hanging in the hall behind you."

"We should check the house first," Hans said.

They made a rapid but somewhat cursory search. Hans found a wall safe in the study but there was no sign of a key. He had the distasteful job of checking Peter's pockets and soon found the right bunch. There were several banknotes, the Humber's logbook and a Dutch passport belonging to Mörz inside the safe.

Hans held up the document and smiled. "One step closer."

Stanley pocketed the passport and searched the basement. There he found a well-equipped and cleverly hidden radio communications station with a three-rotor Enigma encoding machine. They took the Enigma, left the house and jumped into the Snipe. Hans drove straight through the gates while Stanley was crouching out of sight.

After they had driven a couple of miles, Stanley held up his hand. "Stop at the first red telephone box, Hans. I need to report in."

They found a phone at a crossroads near Shoreham aerodrome. Stanley staggered out and returned a few minutes later. "I've told the front desk about the house and the two dead Germans."

"I bet they said you've got some explaining to do," Hans said with a wry smile.

He pressed the accelerator and drove the Snipe through Portslade to Hove, where, despite the late hour, they found a basic hotel for the night. Hans booked them in as telephone engineers on important war work. The night porter was on duty so Hans had to do a spot of negotiating for a late drink and some sandwiches.

Stanley couldn't help looking a bit furtive as they had no luggage apart for the Enigma machine, but they managed to convince the porter that they'd forgotten their overnight bag up on the downs. After a quick drink and a couple of sardine sandwiches they settled down for the night in adjoining rooms. They were both totally exhausted after the day's events.

Hans was concerned that despite having his passport they were no nearer to capturing Mörz. He eventually gave up thinking about the spy and turned his attention to Louise. He missed her terribly and couldn't wait to see her again. Not being able to contact her was tearing him apart inside, but he found comfort in knowing that they would one day be together. His thoughts still with her, he fell into a dreamy and contented sleep.

In the morning Hans reloaded his pistol with standard rounds before popping down for breakfast. Stanley was already tucking in to an extra large plate of sausages, bacon and eggs. He'd clearly lied to the staff about how his face came to be in such a mess because they were fussing over him and paying the other guests no attention whatsoever, which he and Hans found mildly amusing.

After breakfast they drove the Humber to the local police station and handed over the Enigma machine and a telephone number for Stanley's desk sergeant. They then drove back to Stanley's car. As they headed towards the German safe-house, they could see an enormous amount of activity going on in the grounds.

"We'd better put in an appearance," Stanley said, spinning the wheel and taking them through the gates. "The authorities will need to examine the Humber."

When they arrived, Stanley spoke to the chief investigator for a few minutes before rejoining Hans. "They've found a secret bunker protected by a sophisticated booby-trap. It took one of our best men two hours to disarm the device."

"What did they find inside?" Hans asked.

"Mainly weapons and codebooks," Stanley replied with a gleam in his eyes.

Hans could tell from the look on his face that he was itching to say something. "I get the feeling that this might have something to do with U-boats."

Stanley could hardly believe it – Hans was always one step ahead of the game. "The codebooks list their movements and tactics for the next six months. It looks like they're planning on basing two flotillas of U-boats in yet-to-be-built submarine pens at Saint-Nazaire on the French Atlantic coast. They only captured the town a couple of weeks ago. From there they'll find it even easier to target the convoys."

"What will happen here?" Hans asked.

"They'll detonate the charge later to fool the Germans into thinking their security hasn't been breached," Stanley replied, "but we'll get everything out first. By this afternoon there'll only be a darned great hole in the chalk. What a waste."

Stanley climbed back into the car and they headed into Brighton.

"What can you tell me about the Enigma?" Hans asked. "I first saw one of their cipher machines at a trade fair in Leipzig in 1938."

Stanley could barely conceal his surprise. "That was when they were first made available commercially. The Germans have been using the Enigma to encode all communications between the High Command and the Luftwaffe, Kreigsmarine and Wehrmacht."

"I had no idea," Hans said. "Let's hope it yields more

information about their U-boat programme."

Stanley pulled over to the side of the road and parked short of Beaconsfield Road. "This is where we split, Hans. I'll shadow you like at Anson Road."

"And not at Peter's house," Hans said with a wink.

Stanley couldn't believe Hans's composure. He didn't seem fazed by anything, which was actually quite far from the truth. Inside, Hans was a bundle of nerves, but his exterior was always cool and unflustered.

Hans walked confidently up to the front door and knocked.

Franz opened the door. "Thank God you made it out!"

"And you too, young Franz," Hans replied as he followed him inside.

Franz checked the street for anyone who shouldn't be there and pushed the door firmly closed. "My name is Ernest when people can hear," he trembled. He was white as a sheet and still shaking. "I only just escaped in time."

They sat in the kitchen and Franz took the tops off two light ales. "I'm sorry I can't offer you a lager," he said in German. "Sadly they don't sell Beck's over here."

They both suddenly heard a distant rumble that jiggled the light stand and the glasses on one of the shelves.

Franz smiled and banged the table. "That's what I've been waiting for. We had a booby-trapped communications bunker up there. I hope the explosion sent a few Englanders to hell!"

Hans smiled and chinked his bottle. "What are your plans now, Franz?"

"I'm being picked up off Winchelsea in two weeks," Franz replied. "I'll have to report that you finally made it but that we lost the bunker. Then I'll meet up with Peter and Goeppert to get them repatriated."

Hans's face fell and he stared at the table for a moment. "I'm afraid I have some bad news. Just after you got away there was a huge fire-fight with three Special Branch agents. Although Peter and Goeppert were already wounded, they put up one hell of a fight. We killed the Englishmen but Peter and Goeppert were also killed. It was lucky I had my trusty dumdums."

"My dinghy overturned when I arrived and I lost all my equipment," Franz said. "That's why I went for the shotgun."

Hans raised an eyebrow. "How did you get past the beach patrols?"

Franz took a long pull on his beer. "I found a fishing rod and bait box. I even got through a police checkpoint with them."

"You are a resourceful young man," Hans said, deciding to move the conversation on to more delicate matters. "I need to see Mörz as soon as possible."

"I've already been in contact with him," Franz said. "He'll be in suite seven on the top floor of the Ship Hotel in Brighton. Ask for a Mr Christian, but don't call before six in the evening."

"Do you have the financial resources to make it back to the Fatherland?" Hans asked.

"I'll find the cash," Franz said.

Hans removed ten of the white notes from his wallet and handed them over. "Be careful where and how you use them, Franz," he warned. "The British can spot a foreigner very easily."

Tears appeared in Franz's eyes. "How can I thank you?"

"Just tell Admiral Canaris and Kaltenbrunner that the communications bunker was destroyed," Hans said. He checked his watch and inhaled sharply. "Now, young man, I must go. Have a safe trip home."

Franz nodded and saluted sharply. "Heil Hitler!"

Hans merely nodded and left the house.

CHAPTER 9

Comeuppance

Hans once again covered plenty of ground after leaving the flat to make sure he wasn't being tailed. He eventually joined an impatient Stanley in his car two streets away. "Mörz is staying at The Ship."

Stanley gave a low whistle. "Clever bastard. No one would think to look for him there. The suites on the top floor are nice and expensive."

"Which means they're also private," Hans said.

"How are we going to prise him out?" Stanley asked.

Hans rubbed his chin. "There might be a linen chute from the suite down to the hotel laundry room. Most of the bigger hotels I've stayed in have them. If I can overpower him, I'll drop the body down the chute and you can collect him."

Stanley nodded in admiration. "You are the most devious chap I've ever come across, but I'm not happy about leaving you alone with Mörz."

"I'm quite capable," Hans said with a nod towards his Walther.

Stanley still wasn't sure it was a good idea but if he raised any objections he knew Hans would only come back with a solution. "I'll familiarise myself with The Ship's layout, the laundry room in particular," he said, glancing at his watch. "I want to go in at 1800 hours, so we don't have much time. First, we need a hardware shop for some sash cord."

They soon found a suitable shop and Hans bought twenty

yards of cord. He turned round to see Stanley with a large felling axe but waited until he'd put it in the boot of the car before raising the subject.

Stanley's mischievous eyes narrowed. "Let's just say it's a future investment, a 'be prepared' thing," he said mysteriously.

"I didn't know you were a boy scout," Hans said dryly. "Join the club. Now, let's get to the hotel and choose our rendezvous."

The Ship Hotel was an imposing edifice opposite the seafront. Its grey walls were spattered with spots of salt that had been left after spray from the Channel had evaporated and the windows were streaked with rain.

After a brief survey, Stanley found that the most likely access to the laundry bay was down a ramp behind the hotel. "I can't see it being manned during the evening," he said as they pulled up to the seafront like tourists. "Our rendezvous will be a hundred metres to the right of the laundry entrance on the corner of the street.

Hans checked over his shoulder and nodded. "There's plenty of parking."

Stanley then drove round behind the hotel and clapped Hans on the shoulder. "A cornered beast is the most dangerous so be careful, old boy."

Hans climbed out of the car and winked. "I'll kill time until 1800."

He decided there was no point wandering around trying to find a café when he could have a pot of tea and some sandwiches in the hotel. He casually strolled in and found a seat in the pleasant but old-fashioned dining room next to reception. It was sprinkled with elderly people and a handful of naval officers. It gave him good coverage of the ground floor, however, and he made a careful note of the exits in case things went wrong and he had to make a break for it.

The waitresses wore funny little starched white hats that were similar to those worn by domestic servants in Denmark in bygone times. Hans's coffee order was met with a shrug so he settled for a pot of tea and some sandwiches. The sandwiches were awful and he was about to say something before he remembered there was a war on.

Every time he was faced with a dangerous situation he took his mind off the confrontation by focusing on little irrelevances. This time it was the sandwiches, and the old ladies in the dining room smelling of lavender and enjoying their afternoon tea as if they hadn't a care in the world. He decided they must be wealthy middle-class women who viewed teatime as an important daily ritual and an excuse to dress up. They all wore hats bearing the vestiges of Victoria's reign that were completely different from those worn by German women.

Hans's tea soon went cold so he ordered another pot. The waitresses were far too busy to engage in conversation but he felt the management had got the balance about right. He guessed they only earned a pittance but they were well turned out and seemed happy. The only thing that seemed out of place was a man sitting on his own at a table to Hans's left. Hans was careful to avoid eye contact but committed the man's face, build and clothes to memory.

At around six o'clock Hans left the tearoom. He crossed the foyer and took the stairs to the second floor rather than the lift. He then slipped into a poorly lit alcove and waited to see if the other man followed. Sure enough, the man from the tearoom came past in a bit of a hurry. He must have thought that Hans had continued up the stairs, but Hans had reversed their roles and he was now following.

Hans could hear his laboured breathing so he was obviously finding the stairs hard work. Hans, on the other hand, was still fit from the hard labour on the Walraven farm. He'd even managed to stay in shape during his incarceration by making sure he exercised every day. He was also thankful that the thick carpet masked his footfalls. He drew his Walther and quietly moved in behind the other man until he was only ten feet away.

The man suddenly whirled and went for his gun, a look of abject surprise on his face when he found himself staring down the barrel of the Walther. He stopped in his tracks and wisely left his gun in its holster.

Thankful that no one else was in the corridor, Hans raised the Walther and waved it to the right. He then followed the man to a fire exit at the far end. He ushered him through until they came to a flight of stairs.

"Stop!" Hans barked in German. "Let me see some identity."

The man carefully took out his wallet and gave Hans his passport, his eyes absorbing every detail of the standoff.

Hans kept the Walther levelled at his chest and checked the document. "Henri Blok from Roermond in Holland," he muttered with feigned relief. He handed the passport back and put the Walther away. "Let's take the lift, Henri, it's much easier." Although he was calm on the outside, Hans was feeling the pressure now. A bead of perspiration formed on his brow and rolled into his eye. He quickly wiped it away so Henri couldn't tell he was nervous.

Henri led him to suite seven on the top floor and knocked gently on the door.

A tall, heavily built and unattractive man with a sallow complexion and dark rings under his eyes opened the door.

"Wilhelm Mörz," Hans said softly. "You've no idea how pleased I am to see you."

Mörz said nothing as he stepped to one side to allow Hans in. "Tell me, Henri," he said eventually, "why are you arriving together?"

Henri's face fell with shame. "Hans jumped me on the second floor."

"Then you're a blithering dolt," Mörz said caustically before turning to Hans. "I knew you'd be smooth but besting Henri takes some doing."

Hans fixed Henri with a disarming smile. "There was nothing to it really."

Mörz then led Hans into a comfortable drawing room with several armchairs grouped around an unlit open fire. "Please sit down," he said, although it sounded more like an order than an invitation.

Hans noticed that Henri had followed them through, which suited him perfectly. Without wasting any more time, he whipped out the Walther and trained it on Mörz. "Keep your hands where I can see them! Henri, sit in that chair." Hans motioned Mörz to move closer to Henri. "Put your hands behind your back. One false move and you eat a dumdum. Now, Henri, I hope you paid attention to your knots in the Hitler Youth. Tie his wrists firmly behind him. If I think he'll be able to squirm free, you'll meet Mr Dumdum."

Henri used about half the cord and seemed to be making a good job of it judging by Mörz's complaints about being bound too tightly.

Hans couldn't care less that his hands were now chalk white. "Burn off the surplus cord with your lighter."

Henri looked at Hans in surprise. "How do you know I smoke?"

Hans smiled thinly. "I can smell it on your breath and you have little brown smudges between your fingers from the tar."

Henri pulled out a Colibri lighter, his eyes darker than a storm cloud.

"Not too close to the knot, Henri," Hans said. "And put some saliva on the ends to stop them smouldering."

Hans then bound Henri's wrists and ankles behind his back until he was sure he couldn't go anywhere. He shepherded Mörz into the bathroom and pushed him into the bathtub with a powerful shoulder barge. Unfortunately for Mörz, he lost a couple of teeth on the enamel and started to feel a little sorry for himself.

Hans didn't care that his blood was staining the bath because it could be washed away in an instant. "If you move, I'll execute you."

"You wouldn't dare," Mörz hissed through his shattered mouth.

Hans thought it a little odd that Mörz spoke German like a Dutchman, but he put it down to him having spent so much time in Holland. "Don't try me, Mörz. You wouldn't be the first."

Hans slipped out of the suite and quickly found the chambermaids' room next to suite six. It was unlocked and the mouth of the linen chute was at the back. He returned to Mörz, who was clearly extremely uncomfortable. He pulled him out of the bathtub and marched him to the chambermaids' room. He closed the door and pushed Mörz towards the chute, but Mörz steadfastly refused to dive in.

Hans smacked him hard on the temple with the butt of his automatic and Mörz slumped forward. Hans then lifted his legs and heaved him into the chute and he disappeared with a dull rumble. Hans wondered how fast he was travelling when he hit the bottom and decided that the impact probably wasn't survivable. (He didn't know then that the chute curved slightly and that Mörz was ejected into a huge pile of bed linen.)

Stanley was waiting for a body but even he was surprised by how fast Mörz shot out of the chute. He was unconscious so Stanley lifted him onto a trolley, covered him with loose linen and wheeled him out to the car. He glanced up and down the street to make sure no one was watching and then struggled to manhandle Mörz's deadweight into the back seat. He was drenched in sweat by the time he'd finished. Thankfully he didn't have to wait long for Hans. The two men merely nodded at each other as Hans jumped into the passenger seat.

Stanley shifted the car into gear and drove off. Only then did he breathe a sigh of relief. "You had me worried for a bit, Hans."

"I had a few loose ends to tie up," Hans replied casually. "Where are we heading?"

"For a friend's pig farm just south of Horsham," Stanley said. "We'll take the London Road."

It was getting late and traffic was almost non-existent but it still took nearly forty-five minutes to reach the farm. Stanley jumped out to open the gate and then pulled over when they came to a copse halfway up the drive.

"Help me carry Mörz into the trees," he whispered.

They found it relatively easy to move Mörz as he was mobile, although, for obvious reasons, he wasn't terribly talkative. Despite this, by the time they reached the copse they were both breathing hard and perspiration was running down their cheeks.

Stanley pushed the spy onto his back. "Grab the felling axe, Hans."

Hans went back to the car and removed the axe from the boot. He handed the heavy tool to Stanley. "Are you sure you want to do this, Stanley?"

"Go and sit in the car, Hans," he replied firmly.

Despite all the horrors and bloodshed of the past few months, Hans felt a sickening feeling in the pit of his stomach. But then he thought of all the people Mörz had betrayed and condemned to death in Czechoslovakia, Holland and Denmark, and his steely resolve blotted out all compassion for this mass murderer.

Stanley returned to the car about twenty minutes later. He was ashen faced and breathing heavily. "Sorry to drag you into this. That was the most unpleasant thing I've ever done."

"At least the pigs will enjoy their treat," Hans said quietly.

Stanley nodded slowly. "I didn't know whether I could do it but every blow felt like revenge for my wife's death."

Hans didn't say anything at first but, as they drove off, he noticed in the reflection of the rear-view mirror that his friend's face was streaked with tears. "Do you want to talk about it?" he asked softly.

"I lost her in one of the first raids on London," Stanley replied. "She was six moths pregnant with our first child. They asked me if I wanted to know the sex of the child but I couldn't bear the thought of her being cut open. Tonight seemed like a strange form of therapy."

The two men hardly spoke until they drew up outside Hans's flat at Clanricarde Gardens. Hans could see from the interior light that Stanley was still upset. "Come on, my friend, you need a drink."

Stanley followed Hans inside and gratefully accepted a large whisky. "Cheers, Hans," he said as they clinked glasses. "Sadly, this is where you and I part company. Working with you was a privilege. Our little operation couldn't have succeeded without you. I'm afraid the details must remain absolutely confidential or we could both find ourselves in a lot of trouble."

"It's a pity that Mörz's disappearance will have to remain a mystery," Hans said with a glint in his eye. "Maybe one day the story will get told."

Stanley shrugged. "I'll arrange for the department to deal with our friend at The Ship in the morning. Do you mind if I sleep on your sofa tonight?"

Hans checked his watch and grabbed a spare sheet from the airing cupboard. "There's not much of the night left."

They woke at around ten in the morning and had a breakfast of ham and eggs. The events of the previous evening seemed a distant memory already. It was strange how sleep dulled the senses. Hans knew he'd never forget what had happened but realised time would eventually heal the physical wounds and mental scars.

"What would you like to do now?" Stanley asked between mouthfuls. "I should be able to arrange for you to take your pick from any number of assignments."

Hans sipped his tea to give him a moment to think. "I was born to be a pilot, Stanley. I'd like to join a Hurricane or Spitfire squadron so that I can keep fighting the Krauts."

Stanley finished his breakfast and held out his hand. "I wish you every success."

"I can't help thinking about the one that got away," Hans said suddenly.

Stanley frowned. "Who, exactly?"

"I was mistaken for Mörz's contact," Hans said. "The real spy must still be out there somewhere."

"Providing he made it into the country," Stanley reminded him.

"Surely he's worth pursuing," Hans said.

Stanley clapped him on the shoulders. "You've done enough. Let us worry about him." He smiled once more and winked. "It's been a pleasure knowing you, Hans Gundelach."

Hans bowed with uncharacteristic modesty. "And you too, sir."

Their farewells said, Hans felt a curtain of depression enveloping him. The past weeks had been an adrenalin rush of exhilarating highs and despairing lows but if it was all over it felt like such an anti-climax.

Over the next few days he settled in to a humdrum routine and waited for the authorities to contact him. The contrast between this period of quiet and all that action was almost unbearable but Hans hoped there would be more work to come. In the meantime, he smartened up the flat with a bit of DIY and busied himself with thoughts of Louise.

One morning he received an envelope from the Danish Embassy in London containing a letter from his mother. It had been smuggled out of Denmark and into Sweden. She was cleverly unspecific, saying that her sister was keeping well, that Hans's father still smoked Holstebro cigars, and that they were enjoying cycling in the countryside. Hans thought about returning home but there were other priorities now.

The news from occupied Denmark briefly lifted his spirits but he longed for action and adventure.

CHAPTER 10

Flying at last

Several weeks after parting company with Stanley, a brown envelope marked 'On His Majesty's Service' was delivered to Hans by the postman. The letter ordered him to report to RAF Cardington, Section Ind, Hut 3 at the earliest opportunity. He was not allowed to bring any personal effects except a wristwatch, his identity papers and his ration books.

Hans returned his suitcase to Victoria Station's left luggage department and spent most of the following day getting to Cardington in Bedfordshire using public transport. When he arrived, he was surprised to find two vast airship hangars on the base. His induction interview was spread over two days but Hans soon realised that they knew everything about him, including his unauthorised flight across the Channel.

He was given the temporary rank of pilot officer and fitted with a uniform and all the kit, which included a rail ticket to RAF Leuchars in Scotland. The rail journey was interminable and when he eventually arrived he felt hungry and dirty. He reported to the RAF Movement Office at the station and they arranged for a driver to take him to the base at Leuchars. The officers' mess and living quarters seemed quite comfortable and after a hearty instant meal of beef stew and dumplings in an empty mess hall, he took to his room for a much-needed shower and rest.

After breakfast the following day, Hans was told to attend a lecture. He was handed a notebook and a couple of pencils and given details of where to board a bus. He found a group of about fifteen other trainee pilot officers waiting at the stop. After a short ride, they disembarked next to what looked like a Methodist chapel, which was obviously being used as a temporary lecture theatre.

What followed was an introduction to the Hurricane MK2C. Hans was impressed with the improvements they'd made when comparing it with the now familiar MK1. The latest aircraft had been fitted with a Rolls-Royce Merlin XX 1,185 horsepower engine, and it was armed with four 20mm British-built cannon made under licence from Hispano. Extensive modifications had been made to strengthen the all-metal wings and fuselage so that they could take the stresses of the heavier armament and weight of ammunition.

The lectures went on for the best part of a week, after which the trainees were asked to hand in their notebooks. The following Monday, their numbers had thinned somewhat. The next bus journey took those who had passed to an anonymous local airfield for their Hurricane hardware familiarisation. They were each issued with brand new sets of flying gear, helmets, boots and parachutes. Later in the week, they were split into groups of five for flying training.

Hans found the Hurricane an absolute joy to fly. He was mightily impressed with its phenomenal rate of climb, which had been made possible by installing a bigger twin-turbo engine. After one training sortie, he approached his superior officer. "Are we flying with live ammunition, sir?" he asked.

"Not only are you not carrying ammunition," the training officer replied, "but the fuses have also been withdrawn from the cannon's electrical circuits."

Hans raised an eyebrow. "What if we come across enemy aircraft?"

The officer gave him a stern look. "Vanish."

Hans learned later that they wouldn't be allowed to fire the cannon until certain teething problems had been ironed out, but he never did discover what these problems were. They flew every day for several weeks before finding out that they were going to be posted to various squadrons, but they were left in the dark as to where they were going.

Hans was initially posted to Northolt to the west of London, which was a station he'd heard of but knew little about. After a long and boring rail journey south, Hans found there was an underground station nearby. He then managed to get a lift in a Royal Air Force Humber to the airfield, from where he was ordered to report to 303 Squadron. The mess and living quarters were excellent and there was an expansive lawn sloping down to the runway. To his surprise (and a little trepidation) he discovered that 303 was a Polish squadron. He thought he stood out like a sore thumb because he was the only man in a RAF uniform. It didn't even have the word 'Denmark' printed in a small oblong emblem on each arm because the badges weren't yet available.

Hans was also excluded by the language he spoke. The Poles wore Polish uniforms and spoke exclusively in their native tongue. Very few spoke English but some were quite proficient in German. It was another curiosity of war that he had to resort to the language of the enemy to communicate with an ally. Gradually, he came to be accepted. He found the Poles to be dedicated, skilful and extremely brave pilots. They showed none of the demarcation and class differences that existed between the aircrews and ground-staff of the RAF. This applied equally when they were off duty as well as when they were on station.

The Hurricanes were superbly maintained and the pilots were always ready to scramble in the knowledge that their mechanics, riggers, electricians and armourers had all worked effectively to bring the aircraft back to combat readiness after each sortie. Hans was given a short familiarisation course on their .303 calibre machineguns before being given his own aircraft with a dedicated Polish ground support team.

Hans was then allowed to fly a few more training sorties under the careful supervision of Flying Officer Tadeuez Kaweki who was the senior pilot. His Hurricane had the smell of a new aircraft, but he was told it was a rebuild. A couple of days later, he joined his squadron for his first patrol.

Shortly after returning from an uneventful flight along the coast, a runner jogged over to Hans. "You're to report for an interview at Station Flight, sir."

Hans nodded smartly and headed over to meet a Polish liaison officer and a silver-haired RAF wing commander.

The haughty wing commander didn't offer him a seat. "How are you finding the Polish squadron, Gundelach?"

Hans didn't want to speak out of turn so he explained himself as clearly and politely as possible. "In-flight radio communications could be improved, sir."

The wing commander showed him a sheet of paper with a transcript of his communications during the last sortie. "That would explain why you occasionally clarified your orders in German. You caused a few cups of tea to be spilt among the girls monitoring you. Luckily I realised what was going on." He leaned back in his chair and exhaled slowly. "We would like the Poles to use English whenever possible but we have to be realistic. Most of those chaps hardly speak a word of it. Because of this I have decided to transfer you to a RAF Hurricane squadron. Our decision does not imply criticism, because you cannot be blamed for resorting to a common language. I hereby promote you forthwith to flying officer. Fetch your kit and report to the station tailor. I've already sent him the necessary remit for issuing your new insignia. You'll be given details of your next posting tomorrow. That should give you the chance to say farewell to your Polish friends."

The following morning Hans reported to Gravesend to join 501 Squadron. He was to be part of Green 2 Flight but had to wait to be allocated his own Hurricane. He appeared to be the only non-British pilot on the squadron but was made to feel welcome straight away.

That evening he had to drink a yard of ale in the base bar. The yard glass was an extraordinary device like a trumpet with a glass bulb on the end. He thought he was doing quite well until the beer in the bulb rushed down the spout and emptied into his face in one big splurge. The other pilots fell about laughing and Hans had no option but to join in.

"I take it I've failed?" he said with a straight face.

"Don't worry about it," one of the pilots said. "Every bugger fails!"

Hans's new Hurricane smelled factory fresh and was as clean as a new pin. He was told it had all the latest modifications and had only been delivered that morning from the Hawker factory by a pretty female air transport auxiliary pilot. The armourers quickly removed the .303 calibre machineguns, stripped them down to their bare components, degreased the parts and then re-lubricated the entire system with silicone-based oil supplied, apparently, by the Americans.

Hans was told that this significantly increased reliability because the new lubricant was unaffected by extreme temperatures. The guns were remounted and full magazines of .303 rounds including tracer were loaded. Pilots found the tracer rounds invaluable in showing exactly where the bullets ended up. The Radio Corporation of America (RCA) transmitter/receiver in his new Hurricane was also state-of-the-art. Hans was pleased that his new squadron had fewer communication problems – now there was only the odd RAF slang to master. He was also delighted that there was no unnecessary chatter on air.

In their first sortie the next day, Hans's wing was patrolling fifteen thousand feet above the French coast. Except for sporadic flak that left behind a small puff of black smoke, the patrol was pretty uneventful. Then, at a much lower altitude, Hans spotted a small aircraft in his peripheral vision. He rolled the Hurricane onto its wingtip and dived down out of the sun.

As he drew closer, he could see the aircraft was a German Fieseler Storch painted in Luftwaffe colours. The pilot of the Storch must have been pretty surprised to see him roaring out of the heavens and he had no time to take evasive action. Hans's four-second burst literally blasted the little aircraft to pieces and left a fiery trail as its remains spiralled towards the Channel. There was no sign of any parachutes.

Hans had mixed feelings about his first confirmed kill: elation at having destroyed a German plane, but sobered by the knowledge that he had downed a fellow pilot. He also felt sorry for the Storch as it was a lovely little aeroplane that he greatly admired.

As he crossed the French coast he dived down and emptied his remaining ammunition at a surfaced U-boat. (One of the things he'd learned from the Polish squadron was always to return with your ammunition exhausted.) It was an opportunistic target and the .303 calibre shells probably did no damage to its hull but they certainly wreaked havoc among the crew in the conning tower. After his strafing run, Hans pulled up and checked his fuel. He was getting dangerously low so he returned to Gravesend.

After a cup of tea at debriefing, he had his kill confirmed by another member of the squadron. He was then interviewed about the Storch by an intelligence officer who had no interest in the submarine. Afterwards, Hans had his first swastika painted on the side of his cockpit. Bad weather stopped them flying for the rest of the day, and the following morning was still dreary so they were grounded again. Hans used the time to become more familiar with his aircraft. He was very pleased with his new

139

Hurricane but a little disappointed that it hadn't been equipped with the Hispano-Suiza 20mm cannons that he'd trained with but had never fired in anger.

That evening he noticed a message on the board in the mess hall. Flying Officer Sam Hibbert was selling his 1937 Rudge Ulster bronze-head 500cc motorcycle for £85. Hans had ridden a Danish Nimbus for a while in Copenhagen and had a hankering to own a motorcycle again. He arranged to meet Hibbert and found the Rudge to be in showroom condition with only 780 miles on the clock. He didn't have the heart to bargain with the young FO and paid the full amount.

He quickly sorted the insurance but had to settle up by postal order as his bank account hadn't yet been approved. He was free that afternoon and the weather was warm and dry so he went for a spin around the countryside, revelling in the roar of the engine and the impressive turn of speed. He decided to try to find a pub for a pint and a sandwich and soon saw one at the roadside. He turned into the car park at little more than walking pace, then, somewhat carelessly, low-sided on the loose gravel and came off.

He was unhurt except for a badly grazed finger. Thankfully the Rudge was undamaged save for a torn pedal rubber. The landlady insisted on bandaging him up and providing him with his snack and pint. When he returned to the station, his bandaged little finger caused a good deal of hilarity among his fellow pilots. Hans would have to be more careful in future. He convinced himself that he'd learned a valuable lesson about taking things too casually and made up his mind not to let it happen again.

The following day his flight was only at dispersal for a few minutes before they were scrambled. As soon as they were at altitude, they banked round to patrol the Norfolk coast. Hans was just thinking how quiet things were when he spotted a Heinkel 109 a few thousand feet below him. Once again, he dived out of the sun and caught the German pilot unawares. He loosed a four-second burst at the cockpit and peeled away at the last moment.

As he passed the Heinkel, he saw its cockpit canopy jettison. He made a wide turn and saw that the canopy was definitely open. Hans was just thinking how lucky the pilot was to be descending over land when he realised *he* was in trouble. The Hurricane had become unresponsive and wouldn't turn. He tried to see what the problem was but there didn't appear to be any damage to the wings. It must be the tail-plane, he concluded.

Hans had been so intent on attacking the Heinkel that he'd not seen his assailant. The Hurricane was vibrating badly now but he was able to maintain his height. He tried to radio the base but it was useless. He knew he was a sitting duck up here with limited manoeuvrability so he dropped a couple of thousand feet and finally managed to limp back to base. The adrenalin rush overpowered his nerves but the landing was still difficult because of the aircraft's instability and it was a tremendous relief to get down in one piece. He taxied to a stop and jumped out to inspect the damage. Most of the tail assembly was missing. He'd had another lucky escape.

Hans was given a replacement Hurricane immediately while his own aircraft went back to the factory for a rebuild. Hans was airborne again on the next scramble but he was furious when he had to abort an attack because of low engine oil pressure. As he left dispersal feeling somewhat downhearted, Hans was told he had a visitor waiting for him in the mess.

CHAPTER 11

Stanley again

Male or female, Hans wondered as he walked across the infield. To his immense surprise, it was Stanley. He'd never expected to bump into the intelligence officer again. "Good to see you," he said, holding out his hand and grinning like a Cheshire cat.

"Glad to find you still in one piece, despite your tribulations," Stanley replied. He offered Hans a chair and they both sat. Stanley poured him a mug of tea from a steaming pot. "Congratulations on your first couple of kills."

"You've been keeping an eye on me," Hans said good-naturedly.

"You're a bit like a brother after everything we've been through."

"What brings you here?" Hans asked.

"I'm going to whisk you off for a quiet pub lunch," Stanley said, "where I'll explain everything."

Hans smiled thinly and shook his head. "Sorry to let you down, Stanley, but I'm flying as wingman today and, as I've just wrecked my Hurricane, I'm probably in the dog house."

"It's been cleared by a top man at the air works as well as your group captain and various brass," Stanley replied.

Hans noticed the official Austin Six with driver waiting outside the mess. "You have me where you want me then."

"Don't be impressed by the car," Stanley said as he stood to leave. "What I have to discuss is so important that I've been given carte blanche."

Hans was more intrigued than ever but saved his questions for lunch.

In a small office beneath the control tower at RAF Wattisham several miles away, the base commander picked up his phone and listened intently for about half a minute. He then nodded twice. "When shall I assign him to his new post?" he asked eventually. He listened for another few seconds and hung up. He then took a deep breath and dialled another number. "Send Svensen in," he said evenly.

The rural pub Stanley found was very quiet even though there was roast pheasant on the menu. He offered Hans a chair at a small table at the back of the pub and they ordered a hearty lunch from the businesslike but motherly landlady.

Stanley waited until their drinks had arrived before he broached the subject. "I've just heard that a Danish pilot arrived in England via Sweden at about the same time you appeared," he said quietly. "He was assigned to a bomber squadron at RAF Wattisham in Suffolk as a co-pilot because there didn't appear to be any problems with his clearance." Stanley took a sip from his ale. "As you know, we've turned quite a few enemy radio operators who were dropped in by parachute and one of them told his handler that he'd been approached by a serving airman who wanted to transmit information to Germany."

"Was it the Danish pilot?" Hans asked.

Stanley nodded. "It left a few people with red faces, particularly after the almighty cock up they made in your case."

"Did you allow him to send the transmission?"

Stanley nodded again. "Its content didn't appear to be that important so we took the risk in the hope that he would try to send more later. In the meantime, we assigned a full-time undercover security team to watch him. Are you with me so far"?

"Of course," Hans replied. "But I can't work out what this has to do with me."

"The operator we managed to turn is vital for feeding duff information to the Krauts," Stanley continued. "If this Dane tries to pass on sensitive information, we won't be able to change anything for fear of alerting him and we'll lose an important line of disinformation."

Hans suddenly understood. "So this is the guy you were originally expecting! You mistook me for him and brought me in instead. I thought you said that if he hadn't made it into the country he was almost certainly dead."

"I made the mistake of assuming he was," Stanley said quietly. "So I was wrong on all counts." He slid a piece of paper across the table. "The Danish resistance have pinned him down as Paul Svensen from Slesvigland, which is a small town on the German side of the border. Here, of course, he's going by the name of Hans. He was initially educated in one of the town's Danish schools. His father is an ardent National Socialist and the family later moved to Hamburg where Svensen eventually joined the Luftwaffe. He speaks fluent Danish with a strong south Jutland brogue. He was exfiltrated through Denmark, via Sweden and then on to England."

"If he's been here that long," Hans said, "why didn't he try making contact with Mörz?"

Stanley shrugged. "My guess is that they were both waiting to assess the course of the air war. If the British hold out, their primary objective – to disrupt communications – will be redundant. They'll then move to their secondary initiative, which involves the cavity magnetron." Stanley paused for a moment, his eyes narrowing. "We've already launched a devious double-cross to smoke him out."

"Let me guess," Hans said mysteriously. "You're using a

dummy magnetron as bait."

Stanley was again surprised at how nothing seemed to escape Hans. "One has been delivered to his base. They're going to be fitted to all of our bombers in the next year so that they can detect and avoid the German night fighters. We've given him the job of guarding it."

"Isn't that a bit too bold?" Hans asked. "Surely he's bound to get suspicious."

"We're counting on his greed to get the better of him," Stanley countered. "He simply won't be able to resist."

Hans had been wondering for some time who this mystery man was. Now that he knew, he was ashamed that a Dane could double-cross his country, especially when his homeland was in the iron grip of the occupying Nazis.

"These portable devices have to be booby-trapped in case any aircraft crash land behind enemy lines," Stanley explained.

The landlady came and set their plates down. "Bonne appetite, gentlemen," she said with a flourish.

"You were saying," Hans said when the landlady had disappeared out of earshot.

"We can't allow the enemy to learn our secrets so the high-frequency cavity magnetron system must self-destruct when tampered with by foreign agents," Stanley continued. "The Germans will do anything to get their hands on our technology so we're luring Svensen with a dummy device. If he takes the bait and steals the system, it will then detonate as soon as the Krauts examine it."

"How will he escape with the magnetron?" Hans asked.

Stanley made sure no one else could hear them but the pub was still quiet. "You probably heard about the German Messerschmitt pilot who got completely disoriented and landed near Bristol with empty tanks. His aircraft is still being evaluated at Farnborough but it's suddenly become surplus to our requirements as we captured six more in packing crates on a coastal freighter bound for Norway last week."

The agent wolfed down another mouthful. "The idea is to park the BF109 at Wattisham to arouse Svensen's interest. He will be desperate to get his trophy back to Germany to show it off to his superiors. Indeed it'd be a major coup for him and will land him a promotion. You'll then fly in with mechanical trouble and, while you're waiting around for spares, you'll bump into Svensen. Casually mention that the 109 is flight ready because the Americans want to know how it performs. With me so far?"

Hans nodded. "Here comes the interesting part."

Stanley smiled and sipped from his beer; Hans was one step ahead again. "Find out as much as you can about Svensen in general conversation. You'll then drop subtle hints that you are suspicious about his background. Throw in a few questions that he'll find difficult to answer. This will spook him into making a break for it. When he does, you must give chase and make a show of trying to shoot him down. This will convince him that his prize is genuine. In reality, your Hurricane will be armed with only the odd tracer round while the rest will be blanks."

Hans surveyed the wreckage of his superb pheasant lunch. "So you're planning to safeguard your radio operator by appearing to let Svensen go."

"We can't risk Svensen finding out that we've turned the radio man," Stanley said. "If that were to happen, Svensen would report that most of the information the Germans get via supposedly reliable sources is false. At the moment we've got the Luftwaffe flying into traps, sending bombers to useless targets and patrolling the North Sea for non-existent task groups."

"Which is a huge waste of their time and resources," Hans said, nodding. "What happens if he gets shot down during his escape?"

Stanley frowned. "That would be a complete disaster."

"I'll give it a try," Hans said eventually, "but there's no

guarantee he'll take the bait and pinch the 109."

"That's why I need you to panic him," Stanley said mischievously. "The rest of your squadron from Gravesend will have been scrambled to intercept him."

"When do we start?" Hans asked excitedly, the action he'd been hoping for being dropped into his lap.

Stanley glanced at his watch. "Immediately. A flight has already been cleared for you. You'll radio in with engine oil pressure failure this afternoon. I've arranged for your main and auxiliary oil pumps to be removed for repairs so that should give you plenty of time."

"As I won't have any kit," Hans said, "could you please get me a late copy of *Politiken*, the Danish daily paper? It'll be useful in consolidating the ruse. If he sees me reading the paper, it'll unsettle him, especially if I don't bring it up in conversation."

Hans was amazed to find a Hurricane ready and warmed up as soon as they got back to the airfield. He slipped straight into his flight suit and rejoined Stanley by the aircraft.

"Don't forget to check in," Stanley said.

"If all goes according to plan," Hans said, "you'll be hearing from me shortly."

They shook hands and Hans checked the coordinates for his short flight. Then he climbed into the waiting Hurricane and taxied to the end of the runway. He received an immediate green flag so he roared down the runway and eased into the air. He banked round on his pre-arranged heading and fifteen minutes later he was coming in to land at his destination.

"I've got an oil pressure warning," Hans barked into the radio. "I'm declaring an emergency."

"We've an engineer standing by, sir," the operator at RAF Wattisham replied. "Proceed immediately to station flight's hard standing."

Hans smiled and brought the Hurricane in with the odd waggle of the wings and a flick of the throttle to make it look and sound like he was in a spot of trouble. He taxied across the infield to where the engineer was waiting.

Hans slid back the canopy. "I think she's overheating."

"It's probably the oil pump, sir," the engineer replied. "I'll run her up as soon as we can get her on the repair hangar apron." He pointed to a car and driver opposite. "They'll take you to sign out before dropping you to our emergency billet."

"Is this an overnighter then?" Hans asked.

"I'm afraid she won't be ready today, sir," the engineer replied.

Hans did his best to appear impatient. "I've got a war to fight, son."

"Contact station flight for a progress report at six in the morning," he said. "I'll try to make sure she's ready before then."

Hans shook the flight sergeant's hand and was whizzed off in the waiting car.

This is a direct, unedited translation from Hans's Danish notes covering the Svensen meeting:

Being on a bomber base was a new experience for me. There were pathfinder Mosquitoes (the balsawood and ply composite fighter bomber), Lysanders and Boulton Paul Defiants. I noticed the BF109 looking brand new parked outside the Station Flight Technical Wing. It was surrounded by a coterie of admirers, including Svensen. I recognised him by his 'Denmark' shoulder flash as we drove past.

I was shown to my temporary accommodation next to the officers' mess. It was sparsely decorated but clean and they'd kindly provided me with pyjamas, spare underwear, a toothbrush, flannel and a towel, all of which were laid out on the bed. I wondered if Stanley had made it back home. He certainly carried some clout!

There was a knock on the door a moment later. It was a runner with a message from the mess president's adjutant informing me that a tunic and trousers would be with sent over within the hour. Regrettably, there would be no 'Denmark' flash available. He also told me that, as an operational station, dressing for dinner was not necessary.

I found the catering to be of a remarkably high standard. The dining room was unusual in that it was beautifully panelled. I was told that the wood had been salvaged from the mansion that had stood on the site. It gave the place a pleasant and understated atmosphere, and it wasn't cluttered with a plethora of squadron trophies.

I finished the evening with a rarely allowed large scotch at the bar. Svensen was also there, but I spoke to the bloke next to me about the mystery of the BF109 before I turned in for the night.

At breakfast I was told I needed to collect some mail from the office. I couldn't believe it when they handed me two-day-old copies of Politiken *and* Jyllands-Posten *that carried the rubber stamp of the Magazin Du Nord (a large Copenhagen department store). Stanley had again exceeded my wildest expectations. The wartime editions were much thinner than usual but I was sure they would do the trick.*

After dinner that evening I found a comfortable armchair with enough light to read the newspapers by. I got totally absorbed in all the news from home. The country was going through a period of great change: there was a shortage of metal coinage; people were placing adverts for firewood; there were small ads asking for bicycle tyres; and there were offers to convert vehicles to run on Gengas. The Germans were clearly not letting the Danes have access to petrol. I could tell the editorial policy of the papers was to keep a strict non-partisan tone to avoid reprisals from the hated Germans.

I instinctively felt someone watching me. I looked up and saw Svensen staring at me in amazement. "Hello," I said, "you must be Svensen. I've heard a lot about you. I'm a bit busy at the moment but I'd like to have a chat with you tomorrow if that's okay."

He didn't reply and just walked away.

Shortly afterwards, I left the papers on the arm of the chair and went for a game of billiards. I was in luck in more ways than one as I won a pound! As I was about to turn in for the night, I passed through the smoking lounge and noted to my satisfaction that the newspapers had gone. Svensen must have taken note of my loose conversation where I'd mentioned the aircraft being flight ready and tanked up for the Americans.

I was woken at around five in the morning by the duty officer who hurried me to the office telephone. It was Stanley.

"You've done a wonderful job, Hans," he said. "The bird has just flown. Get your skates on and good luck!"

Hans flung on his flight suit and charged out to the hard standing. He was delighted to find that his Hurricane was already purring and fully fuelled – the ground crew had clearly been briefed. He threw a smart salute to them and jumped into the cockpit, then taxied to the end of the runway and accelerated hard into the brightening sky.

"He's trying to stay under our radar en route to Holland," the dispatcher announced, "but he's appearing intermittently at two hundred knots on a heading of 120 degrees southeast. Your squadron of six aircraft led by Sergeant Pilot Toni Glowacki is lying in wait at ten thousand feet just off the Essex coast." (Glowacki was a superbly skilled pilot and one of only a handful of pilots who would become 'Ace-in-a-day' by shooting down five enemy aircraft in a single sortie.)

Hans acknowledged the message and climbed to ten thousand feet for the rendezvous. The grey light of dawn was soon replaced by hazy sunshine. He brought the Hurricane up to its maximum speed to overhaul the fleeing Messerschmitt, the steady roar of its engine never missing a beat.

Hans spotted the Messerschmitt at about the same time he noticed his squadron flying in formation ahead. He quickly joined up with the Hurricanes and slid into position on the left hand end. "Our man is flying at wave-top height," he said. "Commence dive to intercept but do not attack."

Hans then rolled the Hurricane onto its port wingtip and hurtled down towards the tiny Messerschmitt. He could imagine Svensen nervously glancing at his instrument panel in the cockpit, praying that he'd soon reach the relative safety of the Dutch coast. Hans allowed himself a brief smile; the 109 hadn't deviated from its course. He was now only fifteen hundred feet above the spy and moments from opening fire.

"I'm on your wing, Hans," Glowacki said.

Hans nudged the control column over and brought the Hurricane around in a wide sweeping turn to bring him in behind Svensen. He took a deep breath and devoted all his concentration to stalking the enemy aircraft, but he was still a thousand feet away and couldn't fire for a few more seconds.

Svensen spotted him at the last possible moment. He banked sharply towards the Hurricane and fired a quick burst as they raced past each other in a blur of camouflaged paint and whirling propeller blades. Hans gasped as a bullet pierced the fuselage below him and exited the other side. He quickly checked the controls to make sure nothing vital had been hit. The Hurricane responded immediately so he threw it onto its port wing and resumed the chase.

He found he was getting tunnel vision. Apart from Svensen's

jinking 109, nothing outside his cockpit seemed to exist. He bore down on it relentlessly, waiting for the perfect moment to open up. He closed to within a hundred and fifty yards, made a final correction and squeezed the fire button. His first burst would have ripped into the starboard wing of Svensen's 109, his second the cockpit, and in fact one tracer round did strike the Messerschmitt's tail. Hans immediately backed off. It was time to let Svensen off the hook. He knew his squadron would be running low on fuel so they quickly regrouped and headed back to Gravesend, their mission accomplished.

As Hans climbed out of his Hurricane he couldn't help breathing a sigh of relief when he saw the bullet hole in the fuselage just below the cockpit. He'd had several close shaves in the air recently but this one was a little too close for comfort.

Two days later, a secret British intelligence report filtered through concerning the deaths of eight senior German technicians and a double agent when the booby-trapped cavity magnetron they were studying at Wiesbaden Air Base exploded without warning.

EPILOGUE

Hans was an instructor until 1944 when MI5 decided the risk of him falling into German hands after the allied invasion of France was acceptable. His knowledge of the Mörz affair and Svensen's escape were by then irrelevant. He was posted to an operational squadron flying Hurricanes in a ground support role as at this stage of the war the Luftwaffe was just about grounded by a lack of fuel.

Hans found strafing land-based targets with his cannon gave him a sense of power and achievement. When shooting up trains in France he was always careful to avoid the locomotive, however. They were only a priority target over Germany. He found it extremely frustrating that during the Battle of the Bulge visibility was zero for several days over Christmas and his squadron was grounded. When the weather cleared, the Ardennes became an immense shooting gallery and Hans almost felt sorry for the German troops and transport caught in his sights.

With Belgium eventually liberated, Hans was given a few days' leave. He loaded a captured German jeep with food, textiles, chocolates and the like and mounted a Union Jack on the back. Then he drove, with some trepidation, through the forest to the Walraven farm. As the buildings came into view, it was, to his joy, untouched. It looked deserted, however.

Eventually he saw Louise emerge from the front entrance. She looked a little puzzled but healthy, her skin bronzed by the late summer sun. He pulled over and leaped out to embrace her, tears streaming down their faces.

Having composed herself, she turned back to the house. "Hans," she called loudly. "There's someone here to see you."

A small boy appeared in the doorway. He came forward but grabbed his mother's leg as if needing protection. Louise knelt beside him. "Hans," she said softly, "I'd like you to meet your daddy."

Hans felt a surge of pride and love when his son came forward and embraced him.

The little boy looked up with his angelic face and said in Flemish: "Big Hans and little Hans."

A new chapter in the life of Hans Gundelach had begun, a chapter that would never have been opened unless the little English boy had come to his rescue in his darkest hour.

FOOTNOTE

When German forces occupied the town of Saint-Nazaire on June 21 1940, they displaced 40,000 allied troops, 3,000 of whom perished when their rescue ship *Lancastria* was sunk. Between January 1941 and December 1942 several thousand Todt workers built a dock complex to house the U-boat flotillas. The pens were repeatedly attacked by Bomber Command until 1943 when the USAF took over. In all there were more than 50 raids on the port, including a daring commando mission, codenamed Chariot, designed to nullify the threat of the U-boats and the mighty battleship *Tirpitz*, both of which were using the port and contributing to heavy Allied convoy losses in the North Atlantic. Success came at a high price (five Victoria Crosses and eighty more gallantry medals were awarded) as the explosives-laden destroyer *HMS Campbeltown* was rammed into the docks. The mission did put the lock out of action and severely disrupted the German war effort. U-boat losses increased with advances in cavity magnetron radar and sonar detection, and the Battle of the Atlantic was eventually won.

Femhundrede lange Aar
har Slægten baaret sit Navn
virket mangfoldige Steder
til egen og andres Gavn.-
I Tyskland, i Danmark, i Norge,
i Sverrig og bag det rullende Hav,
kæmpede Slægten med blanke Vaaben
og Skjoldet, som Fædrende gav.

Skiftende Tiders Tryk sprængte
ej Slægtskabets Baand.
Sank der end mange i Graven,
dog levende Slægtens Aand.
At Arbejd, at Retfærd i Livet
besejrer og knuser hver spærrende Mur.
Aanden, der hviler paa Slægtstraditioner
ingen kan sætte i Bur.

Tilegnet Slægten Gundelach af
Hans Gundelach Rasmussen . Holstebro 4. januar 1932

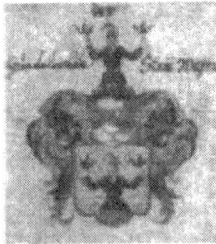

THE GUNDELACH FAMILY CREST

WHEN THE MESSENGER MEETS THE KING

Liam McCann introduces a new all-action hero!

University lecturer and former forensic investigator Ed Sampson discovers that an apparent natural disaster was actually caused by a mysterious rogue satellite. When he finds out that the power behind the incident intends to use a new technology to create a space-based weapons system that will permanently alter the world's climate, he is thrown headlong into a nightmare.

With investigative teams drawing blanks, and with death stalking him at every turn, Sampson follows the trail to the European Space Agency and a solar furnace high in the Pyrenees. He soon realises that the free world is threatened by a conspiracy so terrifying that even the superpowers must face the prospect of annihilation.

Liam McCann's science-fiction thriller takes the reader on a roller-coaster ride and lends itself perfectly to adaptation as a major Hollywood blockbuster.

IN THE LAP OF
THE GODS

Ed Sampson returns for his second all-action outing!

A respected British neurosurgeon is killed in his home. On the same night, a break-in at a top-secret science facility reveals the theft of an electromagnetic pulse machine that can analyse and alter human brain rhythms with terrifying results...

The British must retrieve the machine before it falls into enemy hands. Assigned to the task by their government, Sampson and a beautiful female agent follow the trail to mainland Europe where they learn that a mysterious power is trying to sell it to the highest bidder.

As they race to recover the device, they are stunned to discover that it could be used to launch a pre-emptive strike on NATO forces. With time running out, Sampson risks all to unmask the mastermind and bring him to justice in an orgy of violence and destruction!

Liam McCann's second science-fiction thriller hurls the reader from one crisis to another and lends itself perfectly to adaptation as a major film.

THE DEVIL'S BREATH

Ed Sampson is back in his third high-octane adventure!

While university lecturer Ed Sampson is recovering on a cruise off the Florida coast, the ship is capsized in a category five hurricane. A British Rapid Reaction Force rescues him and he teams up with RRF agent Zoë Fox to investigate the out-of-season event. They learn that the storm's formation seems to be connected to a vast corporation's methane mining interests off Bermuda. With the US economy crippled by a lack of oil, and the mysterious drilling organisation threatening to ration its new power source, time for the West as a whole is running out...

Sampson races to destroy the drilling platforms before a second hurricane devastates much of the southern United States. He and Zoë are on the brink of success when a dramatic new twist leaves them facing Armageddon!

Liam McCann's third action / thriller novel grips from first page to last and lends itself perfectly to adaptation as a Hollywood movie.

ROLLING THUNDER

Ed Sampson returns in this fourth pulsating adventure!

Sampson is injured in a terrorist attack in London that kills one of his closest companions. When he leaves hospital he learns that a Far Eastern crime syndicate appears to be responsible for this and other attacks around the world. And when he discovers that the British government deliberately brought the US into the Second World War by tricking the Japanese into attacking Pearl Harbour, he is drawn into a deadly game of cat-and-mouse with the man at the head of a mysterious organisation that has revenge on its agenda…

Sampson must race against time to bring his nemesis to justice before his diabolical plan can be set in motion.

Liam McCann's fourth science-fiction thriller lends itself perfectly to adaptation as a Hollywood blockbuster.

The Battle of Boxhill

Ryker, a young peregrine falcon, is being given a hunting lesson by his father when they notice a flock of ravens attacking their family by the chalk cliffs they call home. They race back to help but Ryker is knocked unconscious in the battle. When he wakes, he realises his parents and partner are missing. As if this wasn't bad enough, he finds his un-hatched chicks are no longer in their nest!

Ryker pushes thoughts of personal safety to one side and embarks on a journey of discovery. He must unite the oppressed birds in the forest so that they will rise up and help save his family from the evil gamekeeper and his enforcer, Dillon, a raven with a mean streak and foul temper. But Ryker is young and inexperienced in the ways of the world and he doesn't yet know who to trust...

This is a beautifully written and engaging children's story that will appeal to readers of all ages. It's packed with non-stop action, fascinating characters and so much excitement that it will delight, surprise and enthral in equal measure. It has been picked up by Oscar-nominated film producer Bulat Galimgereyev and co-founder of Helix Films Inc., Kevin Foo, who hope to turn it into a feature-length animation.

Liam can be contacted via Twitter: @liambmccann
or through his website: www.liambmccann.com

24049090R10096

Made in the USA
Charleston, SC
14 November 2013